Antipasto Feasts

Other books in the Aris *Kitchen Edition* series:

Grain Gastronomy by Janet Fletcher
Peppers Hot & Chile by Georgeanne Brennan and
Charlotte Glenn

Antipasto Feasts

Variations
on an
Italian Theme
with
Aperitivi
and Sweets

Karen A. Lucas and Lisa Wilson

Aris Books

Berkeley, California

ISBN: 0-943186-40-4

Library of Congress Cataloging-in-Publication Data

Lucas, Karen, 1953–
    Antipasto feasts: variations on an Italian theme with aperitivi and sweets / by Karen Lucas & Lisa Wilson.
        (Aris kitchen edition)
        Includes index.
        ISBN 0-943186-40-4: $9.95
        1. Appetizers—Italy. 2. Cookery, Italian. I. Wilson, Lisa, 1955– .
    II. Title. III. Series.
TX740.L83 1988
641.8'12'0945—dc19   88-14580
                                                                                              CIP

Kitchen Edition books are published
by **Aris Books**
1621 Fifth Street
Berkeley, CA 94710
(415) 527-5171

Series Editor: John Harris
Project Editor: Lee Mooney
Consulting Editor: S. Irene Virbila
Book Design: Lynne O'Neil
Cover Photo: Lisa Blevins
Food Stylist: Stevie Bass
Illustrations: Pamela Manley
Production and ◑ Type: Another Point, Inc.

Contents

Acknowledgements

This book has been enriched by our contact with many special people. Some have contributed directly by encouragement, suggestions and the monumental task of tasting the many versions of each recipe; others have added to our experience both here and in Italy. "Mille Grazie" to Ferruccio and Marisa Sommariva, Carla and Jean-Carlo and particularily Giorgio and Ada Zaffaroni for sharing the secrets of their kitchens. Thanks to Gay Schrag and the kitchen staff of Rapallo Restaurant for all their help and support. We are grateful to chefs Giuliano Bugialli, Carlo Middione, Narsai David and George Loeng for their guidance. Thanks for the wonderful feedback and help from Eddie Pasternak, Warren Galliano, Terry and DiAnn Rooney and also to Michael Ezekiel who did double duty as recipe taster and computer expert. A special thanks to our editors Lee Mooney and S. Irene Virbila and especially our publisher John Harris, whose creative insight and enthusiasm made this book possible. And to the Whale Center of Oakland who donated the use of its computer for this project. Finally, thanks to the customers of Rapallo Restaurant for their years of support.

Introduction

The inspiration for this book came from our travels and experiences in Italy. We found ourselves returning to Italy for the warm, open character of the Italians and their love of simple pleasures. Italian food is as exuberant as the people. And nowhere else is this exuberance more evident than in the colorful antipasto table. The recipes in *Antipasto Feasts* stem from years of studying and cooking in Italy and America and were developed at Rapallo Restaurant in Oakland, California. This book was inspired by evenings of antipasti, aperitivi and friends.

An Italian meal is a multi-layered event not dominated by a "main dish" but composed of courses. At minimum there are two, a *primo piatto* which is usually pasta or soup and a *secondo piatto*, generally fish, fowl or meat. But to introduce this sequence of courses is the lively antipasto table. Antipasto, meaning before the meal, is a collection of dishes, set out buffet style, to stimulate the appetite. It's always a festive way to begin the meal. You sample a taste of this, a slice of something else, sip an aperitivo and relax among family and friends. It can stretch on for an hour. In Italian homes you are served a simple antipasto, perhaps dry-cured beef sliced paper-thin (*bresaola*) or an enticing selection of seasonal vegetables with an olive oil dip (*pinzimonio* or *bagna cauda*). Small, family operated trattorias offer rustic earthenware bowls of black olives in pesto, plump peppers stuffed with prosciutto and bread crumbs and slices of the local salami. Their small tables groan beneath overlapping dishes, stacked several levels high, proudly displaying brightly colored vegetables glistening with olive oil. Fancier restaurants may have a table the length of the dining room displaying handpainted platters as carefully arranged as an elaborate still life. They entice you with fresh mozzarella and goat cheese in whey, gently poached plump red scampi, brilliantly colored sweet roasted peppers in the summer, white beans with tuna in the winter—the selections change with the seasons. There are so many tastes and textures to these room-temperature dishes!

In Italy, though the antipasto table is inevitably followed by other courses, we are always reluctant to move on. We would love to extend the antipasto course to the whole meal, returning to the table again and again. Here in America we find that others share our desire to eat this way, making a meal of small servings of various dishes. By using traditional ingredients in untraditional ways these recipes go beyond the opening course and become the meal. They are the antipasto tradition interpreted in the contemporary American kitchen.

Antipasto Feasts is a personal collection of recipes, some of the most popular from Rapallo Restaurant. Though these recipes were developed in the restaurant they are perfect for home cooking. After all, Italian cuisine comes from regional home kitchens; even the restaurants of Italy emulate them.

Italian cooking is the quickest route from the garden to the table. Products make a quick pass through the kitchen, retaining many of their intrinsic qualities. It is essential to use the best ingredients available. Start by shopping well and a good deal of the work is done. The *Notes on Ingredients* section will give you background, tips on buying and techniques on using specialty products.

There is a chapter of traditional antipasti dishes we have enjoyed in Italy and that have become particular favorites of ours. They range from simple preparations we've enjoyed in homes, to more elegant restaurant fare.

Another chapter contains untraditional dishes to be served at room temperature, as is so much of the food around the Mediterranean. Made earlier that day or before, these dishes have time to marinate, let flavors blend, and are then served at a temperature that highlights every taste. There is a chapter of untraditional recipes that are served hot, with most of the preparation done ahead and only a little last minute cooking required. Split-second timing is not needed which enables the cook to have freedom from the kitchen to enjoy the gathering. We've included recipes for hand-held foods as this makes a meal more fun. We enjoy the casualness of being able to eat with your hands, one hand for food, the other to hold an aperitivo or to punctuate an animated conversation. To close the meal with a sweet touch there are Dolci, some of our favorite dessert recipes, appropriately informal and light.

The Italian aperitivo is a delightful partner to the antipasto table. Whereas hard liquor overpowers food, the lighter aperitivo complements it. Aperitivi can be bitter or sweet; they can be drunk straight or mixed with fruit juices or soda. Imported Italian aperitivi are easily found in most liquor stores. The aperitivo chapter gives background on aperitivi and wines, helps to plan a bar and offers recipes to get you started.

Antipasto has a casual dining feeling that is a natural for family meals. But its diversity of dishes and do-ahead capability make it perfect for entertaining. The key to a successful meal is good planning. It is also the key to enjoying your own party in an unharried and relaxed manner. The chapter *Designing an Antipasto Feast* helps you with that planning by giving ideas on how to choose recipes and menus. You can create an antipasto feast for any occasion by combining traditional antipasti with our antipasto variations, adding dolci, aperitivi, and most of all, a love of good times.

Buon Apetito!

COOK'S NOTE

The number of servings at the end of each recipe reflects its use as a part of an antipasto table. You will have fewer servings per recipe if only a couple dishes are served together.

Notes on Ingredients

ANCHOVIES

Italian cooking often highlights anchovies, a taste sometimes intimidating to Americans. But a small amount of anchovy is often the right element to give life to a dish. When used subtly they add no noticeable fishy or briny taste, only a greater depth of flavor that even card-carrying anchovy haters will enjoy.

For general use buy flat anchovies packed in oil. After opening the can store the anchovies and oil in a plastic container tightly covered in the refrigerator. They will hold for several weeks. To use rinse them under cold water and soak in milk for at least an hour. The milk helps to leach out some salt and soften the anchovies. Rinse again before using. If the recipe calls for a puree, chop the anchovy, then mash it against a cutting board with the side of a large knife.

Whole anchovies packed in salt are available at some Italian delicatessans. They have a fish-like flavor, but not as briny as oil packed anchovies. Rinse well under cold water to remove excess salt and pull out the backbone if you wish. We use these anchovies when the look of a whole fillet is important, such as on pizza or crostini, as their shiny skins and sardine-like appearance is striking.

ARBORIO RICE

Italy is Europe's largest rice producer and consumer. For a thousand years the Po River Valley in Northern Italy has produced most of the country's rice crop. In nearby Milan rice is as important as pasta for the daily starch. Of the more than 50 varieties of rice grown in Italy, the most abundant premium rice is Arborio.

Arborio has plump, short grains and a nutty flavor. During cooking each grain maintains its shape while its exterior starch melts to create a creamy coating. Arborio is used in risotto, the famed rice dish of Northern Italy. We have found that Arborio's distinctive taste and texture is well suited in other recipes such as Suppli di Riso (see page 32) and Arborio Rice Frittata (see page 74). When buying Arborio rice look for the words "superfino" on the package indicating that it has the largest grains. Although more expensive than regular rice, the texture and flavor of Arborio is worth the extra cost.

BELL PEPPERS

Peppers, native to tropical America, have been cultivated in Europe since the 16th century. Like other members of the nightshade family (which includes tomatoes and eggplants) they have become identified with Italian cooking. Peppers range in color from green to yellow to red, which is the sweetest. Pimentos, a type of red pepper, are meatier and once roasted are easier to peel than red bell peppers; we use them whenever they are available. The easiest way to clean bell peppers is to cut them in half lengthwise and with a small knife cut out the core, white ribs and seeds.

Roasted peppers add an intriguing smoky-sweet, almost spicy flavor to nearly all antipasto tables in Italy. They can be prepared in advance and held up to a week refrigerated. Roasted peppers are a stock item in our larder ready for an impromptu antipasto with capers, anchovies, garlic or walnuts; or simply served with olives and a fruity olive oil. To roast peppers place whole red or yellow peppers on a cookie sheet under a broiler or place directly on a grill or gas flame. Cook until the skin is totally charred and blistered. Place the peppers in a paper bag, seal and put the bag on a cookie sheet. Let sit for 30 to 60 minutes to steam the skins loose. Remove the peppers and using the back of a knife scrape off the skin, discard the core and the seeds. If necessary, run the peppers under cold running water to remove all seeds and skin.

CAPERS

Capers are the unripe bud of any of 150 species of the low-growing prickly caper bush. This plant thrives on the heat and arid soil of Mediterranean areas: Italy, Spain, Majorca, Algeria and Turkey. It can be found climbing cliffs and rocky walls, its pink and white blossoms visible throughout the countryside. Capers can be cultivated and are currently being grown in California and Florida. Non-pariel are the smallest capers, capote the largest. Non-pariel capers are the most piquant, most prized and the only ones we suggest you use. As capers are usually stored in a vinegar solution, they must be rinsed before using. Capers provide an earthy, dusky flavor to dishes. Instead of the usual 3-ounce jars, look for a larger size as it is more economical and capers will last indefinitely.

CHEESE

Buy cheese from a shop that not only specializes in imported cheeses but has a large turnover to ensure that its products are fresh. Always ask for a taste before you buy. As cheese picks up aromas when stored in your refrigerator, keep it in a well sealed container. Some cheeses keep for several weeks and are perfect for a snack; when served with roasted peppers (see page 12) or with Crostini (see pages 52 and 84) it makes an impromptu antipasto for drop-in guests. There are many fine Italian cheeses that you will want to sample. Here are a few words about some of our favorites.

BEL PAESE is a mild, soft, creamy cheese with just a hint of tang. Meaning "beautiful country," it originates from Lombardy. We especially like its smooth, rich texture when it is cooked (see Garlic Crespelle with Bel Paese, page 82). Use Monterey jack as a substitute.

FONTINA comes only from the Valle d'Aosta though many cheeses from Europe borrow its name. It has the flavor of herbs and grasses of the Italian Alps. When we are in the Valle d'Aosta we buy Fontina aged and pungent, irregular in shape, covered with a dark brown rind. Since we've never found it in this country, we use a younger version which is a straw-yellow with a buttery, nutty taste. The texture is semi-soft, rich and creamy with a few very small holes. Look for the orange-brown rind that indicates a true Fontina. It makes a good table cheese and is mild and smooth when melted (see Grilled Chard and Fontina Packets, page 70). Fresh mozzarella can sometimes be substituted if necessary.

GORGONZOLA is a blue-veined cheese from Lombardy traceable back to 879 A.D. Well aged gorgonzola rests for a year in damp caves to produce its characteristic blue mold. We prefer the less pungent, creamier *dolcelatte gorgonzola*, which is aged 90 to 150 days. It is a strong flavored cheese that mellows when cooked (see Gorgonzola Domes, page 50). If unavailable use a creamy domestic blue cheese.

MOZZARELLA is a soft, sweetly-bland, milky tasting cheese made in Southern Italy from the milk of water buffalo. It owes its name to the process of tearing (*mozzare*) small pieces of curd to be formed into unique shapes of ½ to 1 pound. *Bocconcini* (little mouthfuls) are the smallest at one ounce. You can find them immersed in a watery whey in cheese shops around Naples. It must be eaten the day it is made or its unique texture and taste are lost. As production is limited, most of what you find as mozzarella in Italy is made from cow's milk, called *fior di latte*. In this country we are fortunate to have a few families making fresh cow's milk mozzarella and it can be found in good cheese shops. Soft and moist, with a characteristic ropy texture, it bears no resemblance to supermarket mozzarella, which we don't recommend using for these recipes. If you must substitute, use a very fresh Monterey jack.

PARMIGIANO REGGIANO is one of the world's greatest cheeses and perhaps the oldest—dating back 2500 years to the Etruscans. Real Parmesan is called Parmigiano Reggiano as it is produced in a delimited area basically between Parma and Reggio. It is produced under very strict controls and aged 2 to 3 years. It can be identified by the name Parmigiano Reggiano stamped into the rind. Although some neighboring provinces produce an almost identical cheese, by law it cannot use the name. It is called *grana*, as is any other dry grating cheese in Italy. Small producers often leave giant wheels of Parmigiano Reggiano with their local bank as collateral against working capital while the cheese ages enough to be sold. The finished product is straw colored, crumbly, slightly salty and strong flavored. Cheese shops in Italy pry chunks from a wheel with a spade shaped chisel and families use this expensive cheese to nibble before a meal or grate over pasta at the table. A less expensive *grana* cheese is used in cooking. Use an Italian *grana* or an Argentinian Reggianito when mixing the cheese with other ingredients as in stuffings, fillings, etc. Use Parmigiano Reggiano for grating over soups, salads or pastas when the taste will show off. With any Parmesan grate it only as you need it; once grated it quickly loses its flavor.

RICOTTA is made from the whey leftover from making another cheese, generally mozzarella. It is fresh, unsalted, soft and moist. Ricotta should be eaten as fresh as possible or its sweetness begins to fade, then sour. Factory-made ricotta found in supermarkets are made with stabilizers and are firmer and drier than fresh. Better cheese shops should carry a ricotta produced by a local cheesemaker or a fresh ricotta shipped from New York or Los Angeles. Taste the brands available to you and choose the sweetest. Cottage cheese will not work as a substitute.

CITRUS ZEST

Zest is the outer, colored skin of any citrus fruit: lemons, oranges, tangerines, limes, grapefruit, etc. The flavor of the fruit is more concentrated in the skin than in the juice and gives an excellent spark to many dishes. Do not include any of the white pith under the skin or the dish will be bitter. It is easiest to obtain the zest from the fruit before juicing it. Use a zester (available in culinary stores), a fine grater or a vegetable peeler. When using a peeler remove the outer skin in strips, cut it into very thin slivers and chop finely.

GARLIC

Although garlic is used throughout Italy it is used differently from area to area. In the North, near France, garlic is used to flavor cooking oils but not found in the dish itself; whereas in Sicily we have been served raw, chopped garlic as a condiment to grilled swordfish. We vary our method of preparing garlic depending on the desired result: For a subtle garlic taste in delicate dishes, heat a peeled clove in the cooking oil and discard it when it starts to brown; Chopped garlic, sautéed to golden brown, will give an earthy taste to a dish; For a bold but not raw taste blanch the cloves for several minutes before chopping; Garlic has a mild sweet, aromatic taste when roasted or baked (see page 83).

Buy garlic that has full, plump, firm cloves. Store it in a place with good air circulation. Peel garlic by separating the cloves, giving them a light rap with the side of a large knife and pulling off the skin with your fingers or a small knife. Peeled whole cloves can be stored in light olive oil for up to a week. Finely chopped garlic can be stored, completely covered by olive oil, for 1 to 2 days.

Garlic Oil

Garlic oil is the wonderful by-product of storing whole cloves in olive oil. The olive oil picks up the piquant aroma and taste of the garlic. If you don't have this oil on hand, slightly crush 8 large peeled garlic cloves and cover with ½ cup of light olive oil. Keep covered at room temperature for at least one hour. Strain before using. (Refrigerated, this oil will last for months.)

HERBS

The taste of fresh herbs is the taste of Italy to us. With the possible exception of olive oil, no other taste sends our memory back so readily to meals eaten there. Nothing enlivens and gives depth to dishes like fresh herbs and they play a central role in our cooking. The herbs that we rely most on are parsley, basil, oregano, marjoram, bay, sage and mint. Others that we use are thyme, lemon thyme, chives, juniper, and tarragon.

There are few steadfast rules on using herbs and often one herb can be substituted for another. Use them freely and experiment with different types; each will alter the character of a dish slightly. Here are a few tips for using herbs:

• Wash your fresh herbs gently in cold water, shake off the excess and wrap in paper towels. They will last a week if refrigerated in plastic bags.

• Flat leaf (also called Italian) parsley has a more robust and authentic flavor than curly leaf parsley and is preferable.

• Rosemary and sage are strong herbs and should be used judiciously so as not to overpower other elements in a dish.

• If you have herbs that you can't use, pack them in layers of salt. The preserved herbs and the flavored salt that results, will last for months.

• If one fresh herb is not available substitute another before resorting to dried herbs. Urge your market to carry a selection of fresh herbs, many of which have year-round availability.

• If you must use dried herbs, remember that they are stronger than fresh. Use only ⅓ the amount called for in a recipe using fresh herbs. Do not use dried basil or parsley at all as they have an unpleasant taste.

OLIVE OIL

Olive oil is the cornerstone of most Mediterranean cooking. It has been vital for thousands of years both as a food and a medicine. Few other foods invoke the tastes and smells of Italy so faithfully as olive oil and there are no substitutes. In Tuscany, for example, a bottle of extra virgin olive oil stands on every table to be used as a condiment with grilled meats, to pour onto saltless bread or to drizzle on soups.

There are four main types of olive oil. *Extra virgin* oil from the first olive pressing is usually dark green, fruity, and very strong in olive flavor; *virgin* oil from the second pressing is medium green with a moderate olive taste; for *pure* oil the pulp is treated with chemicals to extract flavor, the color is pale straw and the taste can be bitter; *fine* oil is obtained by processing the pulp further with water and chemical solvents to extract the last bit of flavor and is not recommended. The Italians are very clear about the uses of each type of oil; a pure or light olive oil for cooking and a virgin or extra virgin when highlighting the flavor as heat destroys the taste. If our recipe calls for "fruity olive oil" as a general rule use extra virgin. If the recipe calls for "light olive oil" use a light virgin or a good pure.

Happily we are finding more brands of quality olive oils available to us in America. Olive oil's popularity has increased due to its distinctive flavor and its monounsaturated, no cholesterol makeup. It is often difficult to guess the quality of an oil by price or by label. The best way to choose an oil is to make a taste comparison with others. Notice if there is a bitter taste of acidity at the back of the throat and choose the oil with the least of this characteristic. A good extra virgin oil should be well balanced with no unpleasant aftertaste (though some superior Tuscan oils have a desirable peppery aftertaste that might take some getting used to). A good virgin or pure should have a mild, clean taste. Buy from stores specializing in Italian products and rely on their recommendations. Ask for oils produced by small companies that can maintain better quality rather than the large industrial companies. Store oils away from the heat or sunlight and use them within a year.

PANCETTA

Pancetta is the Italian equivalent of bacon. It is the same cut of meat, the pork belly, but unlike bacon it is not smoked.

It is cured, salted, lightly spiced then rolled up like a jelly roll. Pancetta has a wonderfully distinctive taste of its own and is worth seeking out. We find that more and more, butcher shops, specialty shops and delicatessens are carrying it.

If you must substitute, either bacon or salt pork may work, depending on the dish (we give substitution recommendations in the recipes). If you use either, simmer for 3 to 4 minutes in water before using to reduce the smokiness of the bacon and the saltiness of the salt pork. Pancetta keeps for weeks in the refrigerator and is a great staple to have on hand. For ease in cutting, first unroll the pancetta so that it will lie flat.

POLENTA

Polenta is a coarse ground cornmeal and generally made into a mush-like porridge known also as polenta. The Roman armies had a similar staple made out of either millet, chickpeas, buckwheat or barley. "Pulmentum" was carried by soldiers and made into mush or a hardened cake. When corn was introduced to Italy in the 17th century it was readily adopted for a similar porridge, especially in the mountainous areas where wheat was less profitable to grow. Today it is prevalent throughout Piedmont, Lombardy, Veneto, and the Fruili. Polenta grains come in a variety of coarseness and color; white polenta is a specialty of the Veneto.

One of our favorite foods, we love polenta's versatility and use it in every course of the meal from antipasto to dessert. As a mush polenta can be made with water, stock or milk. The mush is eaten soft, the consistency of hot cereal, or chilled and cut into slices which are then baked, broiled or fried. It is especially good with game birds, ragouts and stews—any dish where the polenta can absorb the meat juices or sauce.

The traditional method of cooking polenta is over an open hearth in a copper "paiolo," requiring an hour of constant stirring. We favor a more modern method—see page 72.

PROSCIUTTO

Prosciutto, also called *prosciutto crudo* (to distinguish it from *prosciutto cotto*, which is cooked), is a cured raw Italian ham. It is encrusted with salt and black pepper, air-dried, pressed and aged for 10 months to 2 years. We've found that each area in Italy has its local variation of prosciutto, but most cooks agree that the finest comes from Parma, where not only the curing but the raising of the pig is highly specialized and controlled. Prosciutto from Italy has not been available in the United States but due to a change in import laws it may soon be. In the meantime there are some excellent domestic brands available. They vary greatly from brand to brand, even ham to ham, so you may want to sample before you buy. Prosciutto should have a sweet, rich flavor and range from deep pink to red in color. Have your delicatessen slice it paper thin and store it wrapped tightly in plastic wrap in the refrigerator. Presliced, prepackaged prosciutto is invariably too dry.

Prosciutto is best known as an antipasto served with fruit such as melon or, one of our favorites, figs (see Figs, Prosciutto and Mint, page 36). It is also used as an ingredient in many kinds of dishes: pasta, stuffings, soups, savories, sauces and stews. When we have extra prosciutto fat we never throw it away, but use it to flavor soups and vegetables. We use the prized bone with beans and soups. Be careful when adding salt to a dish using prosciutto as the ham is naturally salty.

TOMATOES

The tomato is a native of South America that came to Italy in the 16th century. It was initially believed to be poisonous and was used only as an ornamental plant. The Italians were the first Europeans to accept the tomato as edible and it grew to flourish both in their gardens and their cooking. It was under Italian cultivation that the tiny yellow and green fruit of the tomato plant became red and eventually led to the plum tomato used with such passion in Italy today.

We use fresh tomatoes only in the summer. These seasonal beauties can't be compared to the mealy, pale-tasting tomatoes of the rest of the year. When flavorful tomatoes are not available we cook with a good canned Italian plum tomato—as the Italians do themselves. And recipes that demand the flavor of fresh ripe tomatoes? Save them for the summertime when dishes such as Panzanella (see page 29) are made all the more special by their occasional appearance.

Sun-dried Tomatoes

Sun-dried tomatoes are fresh tomatoes that have been de-hydrated in the open air. Tomatoes drying on rooftops is a common sight in the tomato producing areas of Italy. Sun-drieds have a concentrated, piquant taste and are generally salty. They are available either packed dry or in olive oil. To use the dry-packed tomatoes rehydrate them in hot water until plump. If they are too salty rinse them under cool, running water for a few minutes. Store the rehydrated tomatoes covered with olive oil in a glass jar. The oil becomes as flavorful, and useful, as the tomatoes.

During the summer months when the tomatoes are ripe and plentiful, we like to dry our own. Choose very ripe, soft, deep red tomatoes. Cut the unpeeled tomatoes in half and squeeze out the excess juice and seeds. Lay them cut side up on a cookie sheet and sprinkle lightly with salt. Dry in the sun or on the lowest setting of your oven until they are leathery and dry. Store them covered with olive oil in sterilized glass jars.

VINEGAR

Italian cooks primarily use red wine, white wine and balsamic vinegar. We like to expand that traditional line-up by adding cider, sherry, herb and fruit vinegars. Whatever the type, it is important to buy good quality vinegar. Try all the different vinegars available and choose ones that have an assertive and well rounded flavor. Use a light hand with vinegar, especially when matching foods with wines and aperitivi. The Italian tradition with salad greens is to serve them with a good virgin or extra virgin olive oil and just a dash of vinegar or lemon juice.

Make your own flavored vinegars by infusing white wine vinegar with bruised herbs or finely chopped fruit. Store in sterilized glass bottles. We like herb vinegars on fish and in vinaigrettes based on olive oil. Fruit vinegars are especially nice with poultry, meat and in vinaigrettes made with nut oils.

Balsamic Vinegar

Balsamic vinegar has a beautiful chestnut-brown color and a thick, spicy-sweet taste. A specialty of the Modena area, it has been produced at home for centuries and has had an illustrious past. Balsamic was considered so precious that it was once given in a silver keg as an offering to an emperor and was frequently handed down to survivors through wills. Balsamic is made from fresh Trebbiano grape juice rather than wine which gives it a natural sweetness. It is traditionally aged at least 10, often up to 100, years in a series of casks, graduating in size, of oak, mulberry, chestnut and juniper woods. Each wood imparts its own special flavor. A set of these casks are often given as a bridal dowry. The balsamic vinegars available to us from commercial producers are aged for about 2 years and are much more affordable. We find them perfect for dishes that call for a warm, sweet-sour taste. We use balsamic vinegar in vinaigrettes, over grilled vegetables, to deglaze meat dishes and with seafood. Because of its deep brown color we do not recommend using balsamic in a lightly colored dish, such as a light spring salad, as it might give a muddy look to the final product.

WINE

Wine has played a major role in Italian cooking since Roman times. The foods of Italy have developed hand in hand with the local wines and they are literally made for each other. We keep a dry white Italian wine and a medium-bodied Chianti on hand for cooking. Dry white vermouth (*secco*) has a stronger, fruitier taste than white wine and adds a nice nuance to dishes that are robust enough not to be overpowered by it. When choosing a wine to cook with remember that the taste will be discernible in the final product. Use a good wine, one that you would enjoy drinking. Match the qualities of the wine to a dish; if the dish needs sweetness, use a fruity wine; if the recipe has a light, clean style as do most Italian dishes, don't choose a robust red. After adding a wine to a sauce bring it to a boil for a minute to burn off the alcohol and soften the acidity.

Antipasto Traditional

Antipasti are more commonly found in restaurants than in the Italian home. Homes in the North, where you are more likely to find antipasti than in the poorer South, will serve simple starters such as sliced meats, Pickled Eggplants or Figs with Prosciutto and Mint. More elaborate antipasti are left for special occasions and festivities. Restaurants throughout the country pride themselves on tantalizing antipasto tables where you serve yourself room temperature dishes such as Roasted Eggplant and Peppers or Marinated Mozzarella. Hot antipasti are ordered from the menu and come directly from the kitchen. As in all aspects of Italian cooking, antipasti vary greatly from region to region. Each region has its own specialty. Included in this section are Broiled Mussels from Venice, Panzarotti from Rome and from Sicily, Green Tomatoes Fried with Basil.

Pickled Eggplant

These lightly pickled eggplants are unusual for several reasons. They are slowly braised in the oven which is not a traditional pickling method. The pickling solution has less acidity than normal and no sugar. And by using Japanese eggplants, which are small enough to be pickled whole, they keep their own flavor by absorbing less liquid through their skin.

4 Japanese eggplants
½ cup water
¼ cup fruity olive oil
¼ cup red wine vinegar
1 bay leaf
2 garlic cloves, smashed
2 whole cloves
1 tsp. yellow mustard seed
1 tsp. salt

Preheat oven to 375°F.

Place the eggplants in a small non-aluminum ovenproof casserole or pan that will hold them in one layer. Add the other ingredients. The liquid should reach halfway up the eggplants; if not, add water until it does. Cover and bake for about 45 minutes or until the eggplants are quite soft. Remove them from the casserole and cool the eggplants and liquid separately.

When both are cool, place the eggplants in a glass storage container and add the liquid. Eggplants are ready to eat once cooled but can be stored, refrigerated in the liquid, for up to 8 days.

To serve—slice the eggplants in any fashion you like and serve with savory items such as Sweet Lamb Sausage Bread (see page 66), Chicken Salami (see page 62), or sliced meats.

Makes 8 servings.

Sweet Pickled Vegetables

The pickled vegetables most people are familiar with come in a jar and taste more like vinegar than vegetables. Our pickling solution is gently balanced between sweet and sour and is a backdrop for the taste of fresh vegetables.

In a small saucepan, bring all of the pickling solution ingredients to a boil. Lower the heat to maintain a simmer and poach the vegetables in small batches, one type of vegetable at a time, until crisp-tender. Remove the vegetables with a slotted spoon, set aside to cool and continue until all of the vegetables are cooked.

Serve the vegetables when cool (or store them at room temperature, covered in plastic wrap, for up to 4 hours).

Makes 8 servings.

PICKLING SOLUTION
1 cup water
¾ cup red wine vinegar
2 Tb. tomato puree
2 tsp. salt
1½ cups sugar
¼ cup fruity olive oil
Pinch chili flakes or
    ground cayenne
1 tsp. dry mustard

3 cups sliced fresh
    vegetables such as
    broccoli, cauliflower
    florettes, bell
    peppers, celery,
    fennel bulb, and
    carrots.

Pickled Peppers

ickling is a good way to preserve red and yellow peppers for the winter months when produce is less colorful. Pickled peppers are very easy to make and last several months. They can be served alone or as an accent to other foods, such as Marinated Mozzarella (see page 31), or with chopped olives and parsley on Crostini (see page 52).

4 large red or yellow
  bell peppers
3 cups water
1 cup white distilled
  vinegar
1 bay leaf

Quarter and seed the bell peppers. Bring the water to a boil in a medium non-aluminum saucepan. Add the vinegar, bay leaf and peppers. When the pickling solution comes back to a boil, remove the peppers, which will be crisp-tender. Cool peppers and pickling solution separately. Put the peppers in a large glass jar and add enough of the cool pickling liquid to cover the peppers. Marinate for at least one day before serving. (Refrigerated pickled peppers will last several months.)
    Makes 12 servings.

Roasted Eggplants and Peppers

This is one dish that you find on every antipasto table from the top to the tip of the Italian boot. The tastes are so basic to Italy and the colors so attractive we choose it every time. The eggplant slices can also be grilled.

Preheat the oven to 375°F.

Slice the eggplants in half lengthwise and lay them cut side down on a work surface. Cut into lengthwise slices about ¼-inch thick. Brush both sides of the slices with 3 tablespoons of the garlic oil and sprinkle with salt and pepper. Roast them on a cookie sheet in the oven turning them once. The eggplant slices will be soft, not rubbery, when done. Remove the slices to a cooling rack and sprinkle with the balsamic vinegar. Cool to room temperature.

Slice the roasted peppers into lengthwise strips ½-inch wide. In a large bowl gently toss the eggplant, peppers, remaining 2 tablespoons of garlic oil and oregano. Let the mixture sit for one hour at room temperature before serving. (The mixture can be stored, covered and refrigerated, for a day. Return to room temperature before serving.)

Makes 12 servings.

2 medium eggplants
5 Tb. garlic oil (see page 16)
Salt
Freshly ground black pepper
5 tsp. balsamic vinegar
1 red bell pepper, roasted and peeled (see page 12)
1 yellow bell pepper, roasted and peeled (see page 12)
1 Tb. coarsely chopped fresh oregano

Green Tomatoes Fried with Basil

A platter of fried green tomatoes is a common item on anti-pasto tables of Southern Italy and Sicily. Use the greenest tomatoes you can find as only slices of very hard green tomatoes will fry without disintegrating.

3 or 4 large green
　tomatoes
Salt
Freshly ground black
　pepper
12 to 15 fresh basil
　leaves
¾ cup all-purpose flour
3 eggs
¾ cup cornmeal
1 to 2 Tb. light olive oil
1 lemon, cut into
　wedges, optional

Slice the tomatoes into ½-inch slices and discard the ends. Dry the slices well with paper towels and season with salt and pepper (using ¼ teaspoon of salt for every 4 slices). Place a basil leaf on each slice, trimming it if necessary, so that the leaf does not extend over the edge.

Place the flour in a bowl, the eggs mixed with 1 table-spoon of water in another, and the cornmeal in a third. Holding on to the basil leaf, dip each slice into the flour; then dip into the egg (which will "glue" the basil leaf on); then into the cornmeal making sure that each slice is thoroughly coated. (The tomatoes can be prepared to this point and stored, covered and refrigerated, for up to 2 hours.)

Preheat oven to 250°F.

Heat a large sauté pan, preferably with a non-stick surface, over medium-low heat. When hot add 1 tablespoon of olive oil and several of the tomato slices. Sauté, turning the slices once, until the tomatoes are brown and crisp; add more oil if they begin to stick. Do not overcook the tomatoes or they will lose their shape. Place on a plate lined with paper towels and keep in the warm oven until all slices are cooked. Serve hot or at room temperature with lemon wedges.

Makes 8 servings.

Panzanella

Because of the texture of soaked day-old bread, this Tuscan salad is called Panzanella—"little swamp." We prefer crisp, crunchy bread cubes fried in garlic oil. Use a hearty firm-textured Italian or French bread. This salad should be prepared only in summer when tomatoes are most flavorful and basil is at its peak.

Process the chopped garlic, anchovy, vinegar, olive oil and red bell pepper in a food processor or blender until fairly smooth. Set the dressing aside.

In a large sauté pan, heat the oil and the garlic over medium-low heat. Discard the garlic clove when it starts to brown. Add the bread cubes and cook, turning often, until light brown on all sides. Remove from the pan and drain on a paper towel.

In a medium bowl, mix the fried bread cubes, cucumber, red onion, tomato and basil. Add the dressing and toss well. Let the salad sit at least 10 minutes before serving to let the dressing soak into the bread.

Makes 8 servings.

DRESSING
½ tsp. finely chopped garlic
1 anchovy, finely chopped
1 Tb. red wine vinegar
5 Tb. fruity olive oil
¼ cup coarsely chopped red bell pepper

3 Tb. fruity olive oil
1 whole peeled garlic clove, crushed
1½ cups (1-inch) crustless bread cubes
1 cup (1-inch) cubes cucumber, seeded and peeled if the skin seems tough
¼ cup thinly sliced peeled red onion
1 medium tomato, cut into 1-inch cubes
¼ cup coarsely chopped fresh basil

Fritto Misto
Mixed Fried Vegetables

F ritto Misto, the famous mixed fry from Emilia-Romagna, is a combination of ingredients dipped in batter and deep fried. It can be made with any combination of vegetables, cheeses or meats, often brains or livers. Here we use a large assortment of vegetables, as easy to prepare for fourteen as for four. The wine in the batter gives it a light tenderness, similar to Japanese tempura. Serve Fritto Misto with Garlic Mayonnaise.

2 egg yolks
3 Tb. fruity olive oil
1 tsp. salt
¼ cup cold white wine or white vermouth
1 cup cold water
1 cup all-purpose flour
Vegetable oil for frying, enough to fill a large saucepan 2 inches deep (about 1½ quarts)
6 cups of assorted raw vegetables (see COOK'S NOTE)
Garlic Mayonnaise (recipe follows)

COOK'S NOTE:

Choose any seasonal vegetables, such as red onions, scallions, mushrooms, fennel bulb, green beans, sweet potatoes, and chard stems.Cut the vegetables in a variety of attractive, ¼-inch thick shapes (rounds, half circles, sticks, wedges, ovals, etc.).

Blend the egg yolks and olive oil in a medium bowl. In another bowl, combine the salt, wine and water and whisk into the yolk and oil mixture, pouring in a slow steady stream. Add the flour, a tablespoon at a time, whisking constantly. Refrigerate covered for 2 hours before using.

Heat the vegetable oil in a large saucepan to 375°F. or until a piece of one of the vegetables bubbles immediately after being dropped into the oil. Dip a handful of the vegetables into the batter and coat well. Carefully lower the coated vegetables into the oil with a slotted spoon and fry, turning them once. Remove when they are golden brown, about 2 minutes, and drain on a paper towel. Skim and discard the browned bits floating on the oil. Continue until all the vegetables are cooked.

Serve at once with Garlic Mayonnaise.

Makes 14 servings.

GARLIC MAYONNAISE

To make the mayonnaise by hand, place the egg yolks, lemon juice, garlic, salt, pepper and cayenne in a medium bowl. Beat the oil into the mixture with a wire whisk, adding the oil drop by drop until the yolk has absorbed the first ¼ cup of oil. Add the remaining oil more rapidly in a slow steady stream.

To make the mayonnaise in a food processor, put the yolk mixture in the work bowl fitted with the metal blade and with the motor running add the oil in the same manner. Add the water with the last ½ cup of oil.

Makes 2½ cups.

2 egg yolks
4 tsp. lemon juice
1½ tsp. finely chopped garlic
½ tsp. salt
Pinch white pepper
Pinch cayenne
2 cups light olive oil
1 ½ Tb. water, if making in food processor

Marinated Mozzarella

Since Marinated Mozzarella is so easy to make and stores so well, we always have some in our refrigerator for impromptu snacks. You can vary this basic marinade by adding bay leaves, whole black peppercorns, dried red chilis, anchovies, capers or other fresh herbs.

Cut the mozzarella into ½-inch slices and put in a small bowl. Combine the oregano, garlic cloves and olive oil, and pour over the mozzarella. Cover tightly with plastic wrap and refrigerate for at least 8 hours. (This dish can be stored, covered and refrigerated, for up to one week.)

To serve, arrange the mozzarella slices on a serving plate, leaving a little oil to coat each slice. The cheese should come to room temperature before serving. Sprinkle with salt and freshly ground black pepper. Save the oil to marinate more mozzarella or to use on salads.

Makes 8 servings.

½ pound fresh mozzarella cheese (see page 14)
2 Tb. coarsely chopped fresh oregano
5 whole garlic cloves, peeled
1 cup fruity olive oil
Salt
Freshly ground black pepper

Suppli di Riso
Arborio Rice Croquettes

*S*uppli di Riso *are a common hot snack food in Italy. They are sometimes called* Suppli al Telefono *because when split open the melted mozzarella cheese forms long "telephone wires." Our version is a bit more elegant, using arborio rice, cream and three cheeses. The crispy exterior and creamy interior is a wonderful contrast in textures.*

3 Tb. butter
1 cup finely chopped yellow onion
1 Tb. finely chopped garlic
1¼ cups Arborio rice (see page 11)
¼ tsp. saffron threads
½ tsp. salt
¼ tsp. white pepper
2 cups water
⅓ cup grated Parmesan cheese
⅓ cup heavy cream
1 egg, beaten
1½ ounces fresh mozzarella cheese, cut into 16 (½-inch) cubes
1½ ounces gorgonzola dolce cheese, cut into 16 (½-inch) cubes
1½ cups fine bread crumbs
Vegetable oil for frying, enough to fill a small saucepan 2 inches deep (about 1 quart)
Suppli Sauce (recipe follows)

In a medium saucepan melt the butter over low heat. Sauté the onion until soft but not brown, about 15 minutes. Add the garlic and sauté for 2 minutes. Stir in the rice, saffron, salt, white pepper and water. Bring to a boil, reduce heat and simmer, covered, until tender, about 20 minutes. Remove from the heat and stir in the Parmesan and cream. Cool to room temperature. Add the beaten egg and mix thoroughly. Refrigerate, covered, until rice is cold.

Separate the rice into 16 equal portions. Moisten hands with cold water. Between your palms roll each portion into the shape and size of a golf ball. Embed 1 cube each of mozzarella and gorgonzola into the center of each ball. Coat the rice thoroughly with bread crumbs.

Heat the vegetable oil in a small saucepan to 350°F. or until a small piece of bread starts to bubble a few seconds after being dropped into the oil. Fry suppli, a few at a time, turning once. Remove when they are a deep golden color, about 3 minutes, and drain on a paper towel. Serve at once on a bed of the sauce.

(Suppli can be assembled ahead and refrigerated, uncooked, for 1 to 2 days or frozen for 2 weeks. Thaw, covered, before frying.)

Makes 16 servings.

SUPPLI SAUCE

Heat the olive oil in a medium saucepan over low heat. Add the onion and carrot and cook until soft but not brown, about 15 minutes. Add the tomatoes, their juice, and all remaining ingredients. Bring to a boil, lower heat and simmer the sauce, uncovered, for 30 minutes. Remove the sauce from heat and puree in a blender or food processor. Keep warm or reheat before serving.

Makes 2 cups.

1 Tb. light olive oil
½ cup finely chopped onion
3 Tb. finely chopped, peeled carrot
2 cups diced canned Italian tomatoes, undrained
1 Tb. chopped flat leaf parsley
1 tsp. chopped fresh thyme
1 tsp. chopped fresh oregano
2 tsp. honey
1 Tb. red wine vinegar
2 Tb. white wine or white vermouth
½ tsp. salt
Pinch each cinnamon, cayenne and freshly ground black pepper

Broiled Mussels

Broiled mussels, in their striking blue-black shells are sure attention-getters. They are easy to serve since most of the work can be done in advance. They lend themselves to a variety of toppings. Some are suggested below, or have fun creating your own. The key to success with broiled mussels is to keep them moist by spooning a little of the poaching liquid over the top when you broil them.

For every pound of
   mussels
   (approximately 16)
   use:
½ cup white wine
½ tsp. minced garlic
1 Tb. finely chopped
   fresh parsley
½ cup of assorted
   toppings (see below)
Fennel tops, optional

TOPPINGS

Bread crumbs, lemon
   zest and capers
Extra virgin olive oil,
   bread crumbs and
   fresh herbs
Mint Pesto (see page 73)
   and bread crumbs
Sun-dried Tomato Pesto
   (see page 73)
Pulpo di Olive (see page
   53)
Pickled Garlic (see page
   85)
Chopped fresh
   tomatoes, red onions,
   garlic, vinegar and
   chili flakes—an Italian
   salsa

Cover the mussels with cold water and soak for 15 minutes. If the shells are dirty scrub them with a plastic or metal scrubber. Remove the beards, the tufts of fiber protruding from between the shells, by grabbing them with a clean washcloth and giving them a strong tug. Discard any open mussels which do not close when tapped firmly or any that have cracked shells. Place the mussels in a colander and rinse.

In a large pot place the mussels, wine, garlic and parsley. Cover, bring to a boil, and cook 3 to 4 minutes, shaking occasionally. When done the mussels will pop open. Discard any that do not open. Separate the mussels and the liquid and cool separately. Remove the mussels from their shells and separate the shells, saving the better looking half. (The mussels can be stored submerged in the cooled poaching liquid, covered and refrigerated, for up to 2 days.)

Preheat the broiler.

Place a mussel on each of the half-shells. Place on a broiler pan and top with about ¼ teaspoon of the poaching liquid and ½ teaspoon of the topping. Broil for 2 to 3 minutes or until the mussels are hot. Arrange on a plate, garnished with fennel tops if available, and serve at once.

Budino di Fegato
Chicken Liver Mousse

A *"budino" is a pudding or mousse that can be sweet or savory. This chicken liver mousse was inspired by the Tuscan antipasto of chicken livers on toast,* Crostini di Fegatini.

In a small bowl, combine the juniper berries and marsala, and set aside. Line a 4-cup crock or loaf pan with wax paper.

In a large sauté pan, heat the olive oil over low heat and add the onion. Cook until the onion is very soft and starting to brown, about 30 minutes. Add the garlic, sage and thyme to the onion and continue to cook for 5 minutes. Remove from the heat and set aside.

Meanwhile, combine the celery, peppercorns, bay leaves and water in a medium saucepan. Bring to a boil, reduce heat and simmer for 20 minutes. Strain the liquid, discard the solids and return the liquid to the pan. Bring to a simmer and add the chicken livers. Poach the livers gently until pink inside, 4 to 6 minutes. Remove the livers and discard the poaching liquid.

In a food processor, puree the liver and onion mixture. Add the cream, lemon zest, salt and pepper and process for 5 seconds. Put the liver mixture in a bowl, place a sheet of wax paper directly on the surface of the mixture and set aside.

When the liver mixture has cooled to room temperature, put it in a food processor. With the motor running gradually add the butter in small pieces until well combined. Add the juniper berries and marsala and process with 5 one-second pulses. Pour the mixture into the prepared pan and smooth the top with a spatula. Cover the budino with plastic wrap and refrigerate at least 4 hours or until it is set. (The budino can be stored this way for 3 to 4 days.)

Serve in a ceramic crock or unmold by placing the loaf pan for 3 to 4 seconds in hot water deep enough to reach to the top of the pan. Invert the pan onto a serving plate, remove the pan and the wax paper. Keep the budino covered and refrigerated until serving time.

Makes 16 servings.

1 Tb. juniper berries
2 Tb. marsala or brandy
2 Tb. light olive oil
¾ cup finely chopped onion
2¼ tsp. finely chopped garlic
¼ cup coarsely chopped fresh sage
2 Tb. coarsely chopped fresh thyme
1 celery stalk, coarsely chopped
7 to 10 whole black peppercorns
2 bay leaves
1½ quarts water
1½ pounds chicken livers
6 Tb. heavy cream
1½ tsp. finely chopped lemon zest
½ tsp. salt
¼ tsp. freshly ground black pepper
4 ounces butter, room temperature

Figs, Prosciutto and Mint

*A*mericans are familiar with the popular antipasto, prosciutto and melon, but just as common in Italy is prosciutto and figs. The addition of mint makes this a truly intriguing combination of flavors.

4 ripe, soft figs
16 small fresh mint
   leaves
8 paper-thin slices
   prosciutto

Cut the figs into quarters, lengthwise. Drape a mint leaf over each. Cut each prosciutto slice in half lengthwise. Wrap each fig and mint leaf with a prosciutto strip. (These can be assembled a few hours ahead of time and stored, covered and refrigerated.) Bring to room temperature before serving.
   Makes 8 servings.

Grilled Radicchio and Prosciutto

*R*adicchio, known as the "king of salads," is a bitter red chicory from the area of Treviso in Northern Italy. Traditionally radicchio is combined with fennel as a salad or grilled as a vegetable served with meat. Luckily we are finding radicchio in more and more markets, mostly imported but some grown in California.

1 large head radicchio
¼ cup fruity olive oil
Salt
Freshly ground black
   pepper
¼ cup fresh mint
   leaves, cut into thin
   strips
8 paper-thin slices
   prosciutto

Trim any unattractive leaves from the radicchio and cut the head in half from top to bottom. Cut each half into 4 wedges, each wedge containing part of the white central core, which holds the leaves together.
   Brush each side of the radicchio wedges with the olive oil and sprinkle them with the salt and pepper. Place them on a hot grill and cook until the leaves begin to wilt and turn dark, about 1 minute. Turn the wedges over and cook an additional minute, or until they are hot throughout. Remove them from the grill, sprinkle with the mint and drape each wedge with a slice of prosciutto.
   Place on a serving dish and serve hot.
   Makes 8 servings.

Panzarotti
Fried Stuffed Pastries

Panzarotti are fried hand-size pastries stuffed with cheeses and ham. They can be served hot as a savory turnover or room temperature as sandwiches.

To make the dough, mix the flour and salt in a large bowl. Add the diced butter and work with your fingertips until it is the texture of coarse meal.

Make a well and add the egg yolks, (save the whites for assembly) and 10 tablespoons of cold water. Work the flour into the liquids with a fork, stirring until it forms a soft, slightly sticky ball. Add more water if necessary. Work the dough as little as possible. Cover with plastic wrap and let rest in the refrigerator for 30 minutes.

Mix all filling ingredients in a medium bowl. Set aside until the dough is ready to be rolled.

Roll dough on a lightly floured surface to a thickness of ⅛ inch. Using a 5-inch plate as a guide, cut the dough into circles. Gather the scraps into a ball and reroll, cutting additional circles, yielding 12.

Divide the filling equally and place in the center of each circle. Paint the outside of the circles with the lightly beaten egg whites. Fold the circles in half, covering the filling. Press the edges together firmly, making a tight seal.

Heat the vegetable oil in a large saucepan to 375°F. or until a piece of the dough bubbles immediately after being dropped into the oil. Fry 2 to 3 panzarotti at a time, turning them once. Remove when they are golden brown, about 6 minutes, and drain on a paper towel.

Makes 12 servings.

DOUGH
2¾ cups all-purpose flour
½ tsp. salt
¼ cup (2 ounces) cold butter, diced
2 eggs, separated
10 to 12 Tb. cold water

FILLING
4 ounces Gruyère or Emmentaler cheese, diced
3½ ounces ham, finely chopped
1¾ ounces Parmesan cheese, grated
1 egg, lightly beaten
1 Tb. chopped fresh parsley
2 tsp. chopped fresh herbs (such as thyme, oregano, marjoram)
Pinch freshly ground black pepper

Vegetable oil for frying, enough to fill a large saucepan 2 inches deep (about 1½ quarts)

Stuffed Breast of Veal

*S*tuffed breast of veal is a classic Northern Italian dish. Ours is an elegant version stuffed with ground meats, herbs, pistachios and flavored with marsala. Serve with Sweet Pickled Vegetables (see page 25); Garlic Mayonnaise (see page 31); or Pickled Eggplant (see page 24).

2 pound breast of veal, (1 pound boned), in one piece (see COOK'S NOTE)

½ pound ground veal (see COOK'S NOTE)

6 ounces ground pork (see COOK'S NOTE)

¼ cup pistachio nuts, toasted

2 tsp. finely chopped garlic

1½ Tb. finely chopped fresh marjoram

1 Tb. finely chopped fresh rosemary

2 Tb. red wine

1 Tb. marsala or cream sherry

1 egg

1¼ tsp. salt

1¼ tsp. freshly ground black pepper

3 Swiss chard leaves, trimmed of the white ribs, blanched in boiling water for 5 seconds, rinsed under cold water, and dried

1 Tb. light olive oil

½ cup white wine

With a sharp boning knife remove the bones from the breast and save for another use such as veal stock (fig. 1). Trim the breast of any excess fat or sinew, being careful not to remove the light skin or filmy covering which holds it together. Form it into an 8 by 9-inch rectangle, butterflying thicker parts and patching where needed (fig. 2). It may appear ragged, but it will meld together while cooking.

In a large bowl, combine the remaining ingredients except the chard, oil and wine, and mix thoroughly but gently. Spread the chard leaves over the veal. Form the sausage meat into an 8-inch long salami shape and center it along the length of the breast (fig. 3). Pull the veal up around to cover the stuffing. Tie in 5 or 6 places with butcher string (fig. 4).

Preheat the oven to 325°F.

Heat a large sauté pan to medium-high. Add the olive oil and the veal roll. Sprinkle the veal with salt and pepper and brown well on all sides. Transfer the roll to an ovenproof casserole. Add the white wine to the sauté pan and bring to a boil, scraping up any browned bits. Pour this over the roll, cover and bake until the internal temperature is 150°F., or when pierced with a fork the juices appear clear with no pink color. Remove the roll, cool to room temperature, wrap it in foil and chill completely, at least 2 hours. (The veal roll can be made ahead and stored, well wrapped, in the refrigerator for up to 4 days.) To serve, unwrap and cut away the strings. Slice very thinly.

The veal roll can also be served warm (reduce the salt by half if doing so). When you remove the breast from the oven, remove the butcher string and cut into ½-inch slices. Arrange on a plate and pour the juices from the pan over the top.

Makes 10 servings.

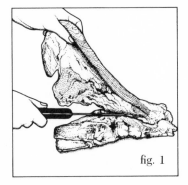

fig. 1

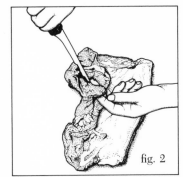

fig. 2

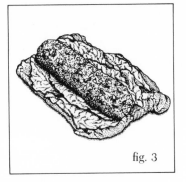

fig. 3

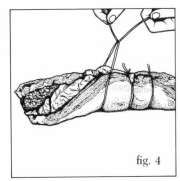

fig. 4

1. Removing bones from the breast.
2. Butterflying the meat.
3. Layering the chard leaves and the sausage on the breast meat.
4. Tieing the rolled veal with butcher string.

COOK'S NOTE

Breasts of veal come in varied shapes and look even odder after boning. You may also find places in the breast where there is a hole or the meat is very thin. This ragged appearance is natural. Just piece the breast together into an approximate rectangular shape and it will glue it-self into a cohesive look-ing whole as it cooks. If your market is unable to provide ground veal, use the same weight of veal stew meat, and grind in the food processor using the procedure discussed on page 92. If ground pork is unavailable use 4 ounces of pork meat, ground in the food pro-cessor with 2 ounces of bacon.

Chilled and Room Temperature Antipasto Variations

The recipes in this section are variations of Italian dishes or use Italian products not normally found on the antipasto table. We have combined traditional foods to make new dishes—like the Capona-tuna (a combination of caponata and tuna). Some recipes are inspired by a traditional preparation that has been updated, such as Scallops in Saor. We have taken ideas from other cuisines like the Scandinavian gravlox and given them an Italian feel. These variations, served at room temperature or chilled, are true to the lively spirit of Italian cooking and interesting to American tastes.

Onion Marmellata

*T*his is a "marmalade" with the zestiness of vinegar and red wine. The sour taste combined with the sweetness of honey makes it a wonderful accompaniment to savory dishes such as Garlic Crespelle with Bel Paese (see page 82) and Crostini (see pages 52 and 84) with Budino di Fegato (see page 35).

2 ounces butter
2 large red onions,
   peeled and cut into
   ½-inch thick slices
¾ cup red wine
¼ cup red wine vinegar
½ cup water
2½ Tb. honey
½ tsp. salt
¼ tsp. freshly ground
   black pepper

In a medium saucepan, melt the butter over low heat. Add the onions and cook until they are soft and wilted, about 30 minutes. Add the wine, vinegar and water and cook slowly until the liquid has evaporated, about 1 hour. The onions should be very tender; add another cup of water and continue to cook if necessary. Stir in the honey, salt and pepper and simmer for 2 to 3 minutes.

(This dish can be stored, covered and refrigerated, for up to one week.) Serve warm or room temperature.

Makes 1½ cups.

Spiced Walnuts

*T*hese addictive walnuts are prepared in three simple steps. First they are soaked to remove the bitter tanin from the skins. Next, they are slowly dried in the oven to make them crunchy, and finally they are roasted with the spices.

3 cups walnut halves
2½ tsp. sugar
1½ tsp. salt
1 tsp. paprika
½ tsp. ground cloves
½ tsp. dry mustard
¼ tsp. nutmeg
¼ cup walnut oil

Place the walnuts in a medium bowl, cover with boiling water and soak for 20 minutes. Drain, rinse under running water and pat the walnuts dry on paper towels. Preheat the oven to 300°F. On an ungreased cookie sheet roast the walnuts for 50 minutes. Remove and increase the heat to 350°F.

In a medium bowl toss the hot walnuts with the remaining ingredients. On an ungreased cookie sheet spread the nuts in a single layer and roast for 20 minutes. Remove and cool to serve. (Spiced walnuts can be stored at room temperature in an airtight container for up to 4 days.)

Makes 3 cups.

Fennel and Apple Salad with Poppy Seeds

This salad is composed of two ingredients—fennel and apples—that in Italy would be served in the simplest manner. By tossing them with a creamy poppy seed dressing we make a simple dish elegant. Use any extra dressing to create your own salads, using celery, cabbage, jicama or any other crunchy vegetable.

To make the dressing, lightly beat the egg in a medium bowl. Add the vinegar, shallot, salt and pepper and mix well. Combine the oils and beat into the mixture with a wire whisk, adding the oil in a slow, steady stream of droplets. Or using a food processor with the motor running, add the oils in the same way. The dressing should look creamy. Stir in the poppy seeds. (The dressing can be stored, covered and refrigerated, for up to one week.) Whisk again before using.

Cut the apples in half, core and slice thinly. Discard any tough outer leaves of the fennel bulb. Slice in half lengthwise and cut out and discard the core. Slice the fennel crosswise into thin slices. In a medium bowl, toss the fennel, apples and just enough dressing to evenly coat each piece. Arrange in a serving bowl and serve at once.

Makes 10 servings.

DRESSING
1 egg
3 Tb. apple cider vinegar
½ tsp. finely chopped shallot
¼ tsp. salt
Freshly ground black pepper
⅔ cup light olive oil
⅓ cup vegetable oil
2½ tsp. poppy seeds

1 green apple, such as Granny Smith or other pippin
1 red apple, such as McIntosh or red delicious
1 medium bulb fennel root

Beets and Cucumbers with Gorgonzola

This bright and colorful salad is composed of diverse flavors and textures—the earthiness of gorgonzola dolce, the sweetness of beets, the crunch of cucumbers. A raspberry-hazelnut dressing brings them all together.

1 pound fresh beets
1 small English cucumber, unpeeled or 1 medium cucumber, peeled, cut in half lengthwise and seeded

DRESSING
2 Tb. raspberry vinegar
½ tsp. finely chopped shallot
¼ tsp. salt
Freshly ground black pepper
¼ cup hazelnut oil
½ cup vegetable oil

2 ounces gorgonzola dolce cheese (see page 13) or any other blue-veined cheese

Cut the stems off of the beets and wash the beets well. Bring a large saucepan of salted water to a boil. Add the beets and cook until tender when pierced with a small knife, 40 to 55 minutes. Drain and cool for 10 minutes. Trim the ends and peel the beets. Cut the beets in half lengthwise and cut each half into 3 wedges. Cut each wedge crosswise into ¼-inch slices and set aside.

Cut the cucumbers into quarters lengthwise and slice each quarter crosswise into ¼-inch slices. Set aside.

To make the dressing, use a whisk or a fork to mix the vinegar, shallot, salt, pepper and the oils together. The dressing can be stored, covered and refrigerated, up to one week. Whisk again just before using.

In a small bowl, toss the cucumber with half of the dressing. In another small bowl, toss the beets with remaining half of the dressing. Do not toss the two vegetables together or the color of the beets will bleed onto the cucumbers. Arrange on a serving plate and top with the crumbled gorgonzola.

Makes 10 servings.

Green Beans with Orange Rouille

This recipe is our adaptation of a garlic mayonnaise from Northern Italy and Southern France. We thin the mayonnaise to a salad dressing consistency with fresh orange juice. This dressing is also delicious with other fresh vegetables, especially asparagus.

To make the dressing, combine the saffron and lemon juice in a small bowl and soak for 5 minutes.

Combine the dressing ingredients except the oils in a food processor, blender or mixing bowl (if making by hand). Combine the oils in a liquid measuring cup. With the motor running, or while whisking by hand, beat the oils into the mixture, adding the oil drop by drop to begin with. After the yolk has absorbed the first ¼ cup of oil add the remaining oil more rapidly in a slow, steady stream. (The rouille can be stored, covered and refrigerated, for up to 5 days.) If it seems too thick after storing, thin it with orange juice.

Wash and trim the green beans. In a large pan, cook them, uncovered, in plenty of rapidly boiling salted water until crisp-tender, 5 to 7 minutes. Remove the beans and plunge them into cold water. Drain and dry well on a paper towel.

Peel the orange removing all of the white pith. Separate the orange into its natural sections, leaving the membranes behind.

To serve, arrange the green beans on a serving plate. Pour the rouille over the center of the beans and arrange the orange sections on top.

Makes 8 servings.

DRESSING
5 threads saffron
1½ tsp. lemon juice
1 egg or 1 yolk if
  preparing by hand
½ tsp. chopped garlic
¼ tsp. salt
Pinch cayenne
1 tsp. chopped orange
  zest
3 Tb. fresh orange juice
½ cup light olive oil
¼ cup vegetable oil

1 pound green beans
1 navel orange

Pumpkin Seed Dip

*T*his rich and intriguing dip uses pumpkin seeds which are not often associated with Italian cooking. However, both in Sicily and the town of Modena you can find traditional recipes using pumpkin seeds. Serve with crunchy vegetables—celery, jicama, cucumbers, romaine stems, green and red peppers—or as a spread for Crostini (see page 52).

1½ cups raw, shelled pumpkin seeds (see COOK'S NOTE)
15 cloves Baked Garlic, peeled (see page 83)
1 tsp. salt
Pinch cayenne
¼ cup oil from sun-dried tomatoes or fruity olive oil
3 Tb. fresh lemon juice
2 tsp. balsamic vinegar
½ to ¾ cup chicken stock

Toast the pumpkin seeds in a large, ungreased sauté pan over medium heat. Stir the seeds every few seconds to toast them uniformly. When they are lightly browned and popping, transfer them to a bowl.

In a food processor or blender, puree the seeds, garlic, salt and cayenne. With the motor running, slowly pour in the oil, lemon juice and vinegar, stopping to scrape down the sides as needed. Add the stock slowly until the mixture is the consistency of a thick, slightly rough-textured dip. Serve at once (or store covered in the refrigerator for up to one week).

Makes 2 cups.

COOK'S NOTE

Raw pumpkin seeds can be found in health food stores, larger produce markets and stores carrying bulk grains and nuts. The jade green seeds remain fresh when kept tightly covered in the refrigerator or freezer.

Fried Chick-peas

Chick-peas, or ceci in Italian, have been a staple in the Mediterranean since 5,000 B.C. The people of ancient Rome so revered the chick-pea that one of the city's most distinguished families, the Cicero, derived their surname from this legume. Chick-peas are mostly used in soups and pastas; however, in Abruzzi they are cooked with chestnuts. In the following recipe we use chestnut flour to give the chick-peas a subtle sweetness beneath the crisp bread crumb coating.

Drain the chick-peas of their liquid and lay them out on paper towels to dry. Place the flour in a bowl. In another bowl beat the eggs lightly with the water. Pass the bread crumbs through a sieve into a third bowl and discard any large crumbs.

Working with about ⅓ cup of chick-peas at a time, roll them in the flour, then shake them gently in the sieve to remove the excess. Next drop them into the egg and stir gently to coat completely. Lift them with a slotted spoon and let the excess egg drip off. Roll the peas in the bread crumbs to cover each pea lightly. Put coated peas on a cookie sheet to "set," about 10 minutes.

In a small saucepan heat the oil to 300-325°F. or until the oil is hot but not smoking. Quickly drop a handful of chick-peas into the oil and fry for 30 seconds, or until they are a dark golden brown. Remove with a slotted spoon onto paper towels and continue frying remaining chick-peas. The chick-peas can be served warm or room temperature. (They can be made up to 2 hours before serving and stored covered at room temperature.)

Makes 8 cups.

3 (15-ounce) cans chick-peas (garbanzo beans)
½ cup chestnut or all-purpose flour (see COOK'S NOTE)
2 eggs
1½ Tb. water
1½ cups fine bread crumbs
Vegetable oil for frying, enough to fill a small saucepan 2-inches deep (about 1 quart)

COOK'S NOTE

Chestnut flour can be difficult to find. Look for it in gourmet markets, Italian markets and stores carrying bulk flours.

Fennel Seed Crackers

*A*nticipating a long, complicated process, not many cooks make their own crackers; however, these are quite easy to make as they don't require lengthy kneading and are easy to roll out. The result is a light, crispy cracker with an alluring, irregular, "homemade" look. Try sprinkling the crackers with black pepper, coarse salt, or cumin seeds instead of the fennel seeds.

1 package (2 tsp.) dry
   yeast
1 Tb. sugar
1½ cups warm water
   (105° to 115°F.)
4 cups bread flour
2 tsp. salt
¼ cup fruity olive oil
¼ tsp. freshly ground
   black pepper
1 egg yolk
1 Tb. water
2 Tb. fennel seeds

In a small, warm bowl sprinkle the yeast and sugar onto the warm water and stir until dissolved. Let stand in a warm place for 5 minutes.

In a large bowl combine the flour and salt. Form a well in the center and add the olive oil, black pepper and yeast mixture. Stir the flour mixture into the liquids forming a dense, slightly sticky dough. Knead the dough on a lightly floured surface a few times until smooth. Place the dough in an oiled bowl, turn the dough to oil the top and cover with a kitchen towel. Let the dough rise in a warm place until double, about 1 hour.

Preheat oven to 350°F.

Gather the dough into a ball and divide it into 20 pieces. Roll each piece into a ball between your hands, then press it into a disk. Roll each disk into a 6- to 7-inch irregular circle of even thickness. If the dough sticks use a little flour on the work surface. Place on a lightly oiled cookie sheet, 5 to a sheet. Lightly beat the egg yolk with the 1 tablespoon of water and brush the crackers. Sprinkle each circle with fennel seeds and prick thoroughly with a fork. Bake in the center or top half of the oven until medium brown, 15 to 20 minutes.

Cool the crackers on a rack for 15 minutes. (Once cooled, the crackers can be stored in an airtight container for several days.)

Makes 10 servings.

Ricotta and Feta Torta

*T**his hearty cheese pie is lively with feta and garlic. Sherry helps the crust stay crisp and adds an unusual flavor. The torta holds well for several days.*

To make the dough, sift the flour onto a work surface. Add the salt, lemon zest and butter and work with your fingertips to the texture of coarse meal. Drizzle with the sherry and cold water and work just until a smooth dough is made; do not overwork. Dust the work surface with extra flour if the dough sticks. Form the dough into a flat disc, wrap in plastic wrap and chill for 30 minutes before rolling.

To make the filling, combine all ingredients in a large bowl, mix well and add salt if necessary.

Preheat oven to 350°F.

Roll the dough on a floured surface to a 16-inch circle; the dough will be thin. Slide the removable bottom of an 8- to 9½-inch springform pan under the dough to help lift it and lower bottom into pan. Press the dough into the corners and pour in the filling. Trim the dough so that it is even with the top of the pan, then loosely roll the dough down to form a 1-inch rolled border above the filling. This will drape over the filling as it cooks making an attractive border.

Bake the torta on the floor of the oven for 35 minutes; then raise to the upper third of the oven and continue to bake until lightly browned, and a knife inserted into the center comes out clean, about 20 minutes. Cool the torta in the pan, then carefully remove the ring and slide the torta onto a serving dish.

(The torta can be made ahead, wrapped and refrigerated for up to 2 days. Remove from the refrigerator one hour before serving.) Cut the torta into thin slices.

Makes 10 servings.

DOUGH

- 1½ cups all-purpose flour
- Pinch salt
- ½ tsp. finely chopped lemon zest
- 3 ounces chilled butter, cut into ½-inch cubes
- 2 Tb. dry sherry
- 4 Tb. cold water

FILLING

- 1 pound feta cheese, rinsed well and finely crumbled (see COOK'S NOTE)
- 8 ounces ricotta cheese
- 4 eggs
- 1 tsp. minced fresh rosemary
- 1½ tsp. finely chopped garlic
- ¼ tsp. freshly ground black pepper
- ½ cup pine nuts or chopped walnuts, toasted
- Salt, if needed

COOK'S NOTE

Most feta cheeses are packed in a salt brine and some can be quite salty. Taste the feta before using it. If the feta is very salty, soak it in several changes of cold water. Since fetas vary so much, you should taste the filling and add the salt if necessary.

Gorgonzola Domes

We love Ada Boni's gorgonzola biscotti. We have based this recipe on hers, adding walnuts—a natural partner to gorgonzola cheese. These filled savories are rich and flaky, with a deep shine from the egg yolk and cream wash.

DOUGH

5 Tb. butter, room temperature

1 Tb. walnut oil

6 ounces gorgonzola dolce cheese, crumbled and room temperature

2 egg yolks

2 Tb. water

2 cups all-purpose flour

Pinch each nutmeg, salt, cayenne and freshly ground black pepper

FILLING

2 ounces gorgonzola dolce cheese

6 Tb. toasted walnuts

EGG WASH

1 egg, separated

1 Tb. heavy cream

To make the dough, cream the butter and oil together in a medium bowl until soft and fluffy. Add the gorgonzola and beat with the butter. Add the egg yolks and water, and beat until fairly smooth. Add the flour, nutmeg, salt, cayenne and pepper and mix until it forms a soft, firm dough. Pat the dough into a rectangle, cover with plastic wrap and let rest in the refrigerator for 30 to 60 minutes.

Meanwhile combine the filling ingredients and set aside. Preheat oven to 375°F.

On a lightly floured board, roll the dough ⅛ inch thick. Cut twelve 3-inch circles and twelve 3½-inch circles. Lightly beat the egg white and brush the outer edge of the smaller circles with it. Put 1 tablespoon of the filling in the center of each smaller circle. Cover with the larger circles and press the edges firmly to make a tight seal. Press the edges with the back of a fork to make a decorative border. (The domes can be prepared ahead to this point and stored, covered and refrigerated, for up to 8 hours or frozen for several weeks.)

Lightly beat together the egg yolk and cream in a small bowl and brush lightly on the top of the domes. Bake on a buttered cookie sheet until medium brown, 20 to 25 minutes. Remove to a cooling rack and serve at room temperature.

Makes 12 servings.

Frittata di Pasta
Crispy Pasta Pancake

Frittata is usually eggs and vegetables slowly cooked in the oven—a thick Italian omelette. Another traditional Italian frittata is made mostly of pasta bound together with eggs. We use angel hair pasta because the fine strands stick together well, eliminating the need for eggs. The result is very light and crispy. This dish is a great way to use leftover angel hair pasta.

In a large pot of rapidly boiling salted water, cook the pasta until it is "al dente" or cooked through but with a little resistance, 1 to 3 minutes. Drain the pasta well, put it into a medium bowl and toss with 3 teaspoons of the olive oil. Set aside.

In an 8-inch non-stick sauté or crepe pan, heat 1 teaspoon of the remaining olive oil. Add the garlic and sauté until the garlic just begins to turn golden. Remove from the heat and add the garlic and the herbs to the pasta and toss. Divide the pasta mixture into thirds.

Heat the non-stick pan over medium-high heat. Add 1 teaspoon of the olive oil and half of the pasta from one of the thirds and pat down flat with the back of a spoon. Sprinkle with 2 tablespoons of the Parmesan cheese. Top with the remaining half of the pasta and pat down with the back of the spoon. Sprinkle with salt and pepper. When the frittata is a deep medium brown, 4 to 5 minutes, turn it over with a spatula and cook the second side until it is a deep medium brown. Slide the frittata onto paper towels and blot off any extra oil.

Repeat with the remaining 2 batches adding 1 teaspoon of olive oil each time. Let the frittatas cool to room temperature and cut each into 4 wedges.

Makes 12 servings.

6 ounces angel hair pasta, dry or fresh

7 tsp. fruity olive oil

4½ tsp. finely chopped garlic

3 Tb. coarsely chopped fresh herbs (such as oregano, majoram, basil, flat leaf parsley)

6 Tb. freshly grated Parmesan cheese

Salt

Freshly ground black pepper

Crostini

Italians are very resourceful in using leftover bread. Particularly in Tuscany, where many trattorias offer complimentary Crostini di Fegatini *(chicken liver spread on toasts)*, you find a tradition of toasted breads and toppings as an antipasto. We keep crostini in our freezer for a quick antipasto for drop-in guests. Top them with about anything you have on hand and serve room temperature or hot (see hot crostini recipes on page 84).

Preheat broiler.

Slice a baguette or any other narrow bread into diagonal slices, between ¼- and ½-inch thick. (The crostini can be frozen at this point, in a plastic bag for several weeks.)

Place the crostini on a dry cookie sheet and toast for 30 to 60 seconds until light brown. Turn the crostini over and toast until light brown. Let cool to room temperature. Spread with desired topping.

The average baguette will yield between 40 to 50 slices.

TOPPINGS

- Italian Gravlox, page 56
- Budino di Fegato, page 35
- Pumpkin Seed Dip, page 46
- Capona-tuna, page 54
- Cream cheese and Sweet Pickled Vegetables, page 25
- Onion Marmellata, page 42
- Pulpo di Olive, (recipe follows)
- White Bean Spread (recipe follows)
- Sliced meats
- Goat cheese, sun-dried tomato and basil

PULPO DI OLIVE (Olive Spread)

Add all of the ingredients to a food processor and puree for 25 seconds, scraping the sides once. (The mixture can be stored, covered and refrigerated, for about one week.)
    Makes ⅔ cup.

1 cup rinsed and pitted calamata olives (about 7 ounces before pitting)
1 Tb. chopped fresh oregano
3 Tb. fruity olive oil
½ tsp. finely chopped garlic
Pinch chili flakes

WHITE BEAN SPREAD

In a small sauté pan sauté the pancetta in the olive oil until light brown. Remove the pancetta with a slotted spoon and set aside. Sauté the onion in the remaining oil until soft, 6 to 8 minutes. Add the garlic and sauté for 3 to 4 minutes.
    In a food processor, puree the pancetta, onions, garlic, cooking oil and the beans until smooth (see COOK'S NOTE). Transfer to a bowl and mix in the celery, meats and seasonings. (The spread can be served at once or covered and refrigerated for 3 to 4 days.)
    Makes ¾ cup.

¼ cup finely chopped pancetta
3 Tb. light olive oil
⅓ cup finely diced yellow onion
1 tsp. finely chopped garlic
1½ cups cooked white beans
¼ cup finely diced celery
6 Tb. finely diced cured Italian meats (salami, prosciutto, ham, coppa, etc.)
Salt to taste
Freshly ground black pepper

COOK'S NOTE

If you are using cold, pre-cooked beans, add 3 tablespoons of hot water or stock to help puree it.

Capona-tuna

What we know as Japanese eggplants are found in Italy as frequently as the larger globe eggplants. Here we use their attractive slender shape as a utensil to hold slow-cooked peppers, capers and tomatoes. This dish is similar to Capon-atina (a Sicilian dish which is an eggplant and vegetable relish) but with the addition of tuna, therefore the name.

FILLING
1 Tb. light olive oil
1 cup finely diced red onion
½ cup finely diced green pepper
1 cup finely diced red pepper
½ cup finely diced celery
⅓ cup black raisins
2 Tb. capers, rinsed
3 Tb. pine nuts, toasted
2 Tb. chopped green olives
1½ cups chopped fresh tomatoes, peeled and seeded or 1½ cups chopped canned tomatoes, drained
1 tsp. salt
½ tsp. freshly ground black pepper

8 Japanese eggplants, rubbed with light olive oil
Salt
Freshly ground black pepper
10 ounces fresh tuna, poached to medium done or 10 ounces of canned tuna, packed in oil, drained
2 Tb. fruity olive oil

Preheat oven to 325°F.

In a medium saucepan, heat the olive oil and sauté the onions until soft, 5 to 6 minutes. Add the peppers and celery and sauté until soft, 4 to 6 minutes. Add the remaining filling ingredients, stir well and bake, covered, for one hour. Cool to room temperature. (The filling can be stored, covered and refrigerated, for 2 to 3 days but bring the mixture to room temperature before serving.)

Sprinkle the eggplants with salt and pepper and bake on a cookie sheet until they are slightly withered and soft to touch, 20 to 30 minutes. Cool to room temperature, and store wrapped in plastic. They are best when baked the day they are served.

To serve, flake the tuna and gently combine it with the filling. Slice the eggplants in half lengthwise and hollow them out using a small spoon. Brush the cut side of the eggplants with the 2 tablespoons of olive oil. Stuff the hollowed bowl of each eggplant with the pepper-tuna filling and serve.

Makes 16 servings.

Calamari and Celery Salad

Calamari (squid) salad should be dressed with a light touch. A splash of lemon juice is enough to bring out a lively flavor but not to compete with aperitivi. Whether or not to leave the skin on the calamari is your option. The skin will often come off during the cleaning process, but if some stays on, we find the dark pink of the skin attractive.

To clean the calamari, cut off the tentacles just above the eye. Remove and discard the hard ball in the base of the tentacles. Set the tentacles aside. Pull the head from the body. Remove the plastic-like quill from inside the body sac. With the back of a knife scrape toward the opening to remove the innards. Thoroughly rinse the tentacles and body sacs inside and out. (Calamari can be prepared ahead to this point and refrigerated, covered, for up to 8 hours.)

Cut the calamari into ½-inch rings. Fill a pan fitted with a strainer or a sieve with water and add the bay leaves, lemon, ½ cup white wine and 1 teaspoon salt and bring to a boil. Put the calamari rings in the strainer in small batches and poach for about 20 seconds; remove and spread out on a cookie sheet to cool. It is important not to overcook the calamari or it will be tough and rubbery. Repeat until all of the rings are cooked. Cook the tentacles for 30 seconds using the same method.

When the calamari is room temperature, combine it in a large bowl with the remaining ingredients including remaining ¼ cup wine and ¼ teaspoon salt. Let it rest at least 30 minutes before serving. Toss well and serve in a bowl or a serving plate.

Makes 16 servings.

5 pounds calamari, uncleaned (2½ pounds cleaned)

2 bay leaves

1 lemon, cut into wedges

¾ cup white wine

1¼ tsp. salt

6 stalks celery, thinly sliced

1 red onion, peeled, halved and thinly sliced

¼ cup fresh lemon juice

½ cup fruity olive oil

¼ cup coarsely chopped fresh marjoram or oregano

¼ tsp. freshly ground black pepper

Italian Gravlox

Gravlox is a traditional Scandanavian dish of salmon cured with aquavit and dill. We prefer to use grappa and fennel seeds as they don't overpower the taste of the fish. The curing process takes several days so start it in advance. Like the more familiar lox it is rich and should be sliced very thinly.

1 (1½-2 pound) fillet of fresh salmon, skin on, preferably the tail end

1 medium red onion, peeled and thinly sliced

2 Tb. fennel seeds

1½ Tb. sugar

2½ Tb. coarse or kosher salt

1 cup grappa (Italian white grape brandy) or vodka (enough to reach half way up the fish)

Fruity olive oil

Trim any white membranes from the fish. With tweezers or pliers pull out any bones left in the fillet (this makes slicing much easier). Lay the onions, fennel seeds, sugar and salt in a non-aluminum pan just large enough to hold the fillet flat, such as a bread pan. Lay the fillet on the seasonings, skin side up. Pour the grappa over the fish. Cover first with plastic wrap, then with foil and lay a 3- to 5-pound weight over the length of the fillet (try a sack of flour, bottles, milk cartons, or a large plastic bag of dry beans). Marinate the salmon in the refrigerator for 2 to 4 days, depending on the thickness. When done the fish will look opaque and taste cured throughout.

Remove the salmon and brush, do not wash, the seasonings off. (The gravlox can be rewrapped in plastic and stored for up to 3 days, or served at once.) To serve, cut the meat of the fish crosswise into very thin slices lifting them off the skin which should remain intact. Arrange the slices on a plate and dab each slice with a little of the marinade and some of the olive oil. Arrange the onion slices on the side. Serve with breadsticks, crostini, or drape over sticks of fresh fennel.

Makes 10 servings.

Scallops in Saor

This recipe is modeled after a dish from Venice, Sfogi in Saor, *fried sole marinated in vinegar and sweet spices.* In this recipe thinly sliced scallops are "cold-cooked" by the acid of lemon juice and wine, like the Latin American ceviche, (raw fish marinated in lime juice). Begin this process in the morning to be ready for that evening. The refreshing, tart qualities of Scallops in Saor work wonderfully with fried dishes such as: Fritto Misto (see page 30), Pasta Fries (see page 71) or Arborio Rice Frittata (see page 74).

Trim the foot (the tough muscle attached on the side) from each scallop, if still there. Slice each scallop against the grain into 3 round slices.

In a glass or ceramic bowl, assemble the remaining ingredients, except the pepper, add the scallops and toss. Refrigerate, covered, for 7 to 8 hours (overnight marination over "cooks" the scallops to a rubbery texture). The scallops will appear opaque, as if cooked, when ready.

On a serving plate arrange the scallops, onions, pine nuts and raisins and sprinkle with the pepper.

Makes 10 servings.

1 pound fresh sea scallops
½ red onion, peeled and cut into ¼-inch rings
¼ cup red wine vinegar
½ cup fresh lemon juice (4 to 6 lemons)
2 bay leaves
2 Tb. pine nuts, toasted
2 Tb. golden raisins
4 whole cloves
1 (2-inch) cinnamon stick
½ tsp. salt
Freshly ground black pepper

Coniglio Farcito
Stuffed Rabbit

*C*oniglio farcito is stylish, elegant, colorful and always the
focal point of a meal. Although it looks complicated to
make, boning the rabbit only takes about fifteen minutes, and
assembling the filling of simple ingredients is easy.

3 eggs

1 tsp. finely chopped
fresh thyme

¼ tsp. salt

Freshly ground white
pepper

1 tsp. light olive oil

1 whole fryer rabbit,
preferably fresh

¾ tsp. salt

¼ tsp. freshly ground
black pepper

½ tsp. finely minced
garlic

10 very thin slices
prosciutto, about 2½
ounces

5 Swiss chard leaves,
trimmed of the white
ribs, blanched in
boiling water for 5
seconds, rinsed under
cold water and dried

1 roasted red pepper,
peeled and cut into
½-inch strips (see
page 12)

Chicken stock or fruity
olive oil, optional

In a small bowl lightly beat the eggs, thyme, ¼ teaspoon salt
and white pepper. Heat a 7-inch crepe or omelette pan over
medium-high heat. When hot add ½ teaspoon oil and half of
the egg mixture. Shake the pan while briefly stirring the eggs
with the back of a fork, then pat out to an even thickness.
When the eggs just start to brown (20 to 30 seconds) flip over
with a spatula and cook until set (5 seconds). Cool on a plate
and repeat with the remaining oil and egg mixture. Cover
and set aside.

To bone the rabbit, lay it on its back and remove any
organs (save the liver for Budino di Fegato, page 35) and fat
from the cavity of the body. Slit the breast open to the neck
so shoulders lie down flat. Remove the first joint from the
front legs. Cut down the length of the front leg bone, shoulder to end, exposing it. With the tip of a small knife carefully
free the leg bone and shoulder blade from the meat and detach (fig. 1).

Run the tip of your knife between the ribs and the muscle covering them, being careful not to create holes. Peel
back the meat to the spine (fig. 2) on each side cutting away
as little meat as possible. Beginning at the neck scrape the
meat away from the spine freeing it as you go (fig. 3). Work
down toward the tail loosening the meat gently until the entire spine can be pulled free to the hind legs.

Cut the meat away from the flat pelvic bone to expose it.
Cut down the length of the leg bone exposing it. Free the
bone from the meat (fig. 4), being careful around the knee
joint. Detach from the spine. Continue scraping the meat
from the spine to pull the skeleton free. Check the meat for
any small bones that you may have missed.

Fold the forequarters meat down over several inches of back to build up that area. Butterfly the loins (round rolls of meat on either side of the spine) out to help build up the outer flaps. Butterfly the leg meat to build up the gap between the loin and the hind leg (fig. 5). The rabbit should now be in a rectangular shape of fairly even thickness. Do not worry about holes, as the meat will come together during cooking.

Preheat oven to 350°F.

Put the rabbit onto a 16- by 12-inch piece of cheesecloth, or parchment paper. Re-form into a rectangle patching any holes. Sprinkle with ¾ teaspoon salt, the black pepper and garlic. In single layers, covering the entire surface of the rabbit, lay first the prosciutto, then the two omelettes and top with the chard leaves. Lay the red pepper strips down the center. Starting with the long side, roll the rabbit tightly over the stuffing using the cheesecloth to help you (fig. 6). Twist the ends closed and secure tightly with kitchen string. Wrap securely in foil and twist the ends closed.

Place the roll on a cookie sheet and bake for 30 to 40 minutes, until the internal temperature reaches 140°F, or the juices run clear when the meat is pierced. Chill well in the wrapping, at least two hours. (The roll can be stored, refrigerated, for up to 3 days.) To serve, slice into ½-inch thick slices and if desired brush with cold chicken stock or olive oil to make them shine.

Makes 8 servings.

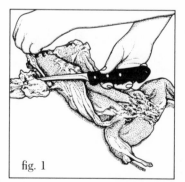

fig. 1

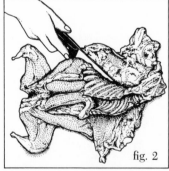

fig. 2

1. Detaching leg bone and shoulder blade from the meat.
2. Peeling back the meat down to the spine.

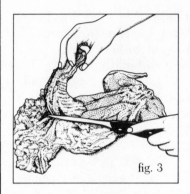

fig. 3

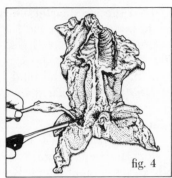

fig. 4

3. Scraping the meat away from the spine.
4. Cutting out the leg bone.
5. Butterflying the leg meat.
6. Rolling the rabbit over the stuffing.

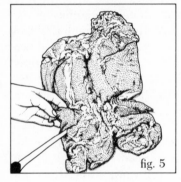

fig. 5

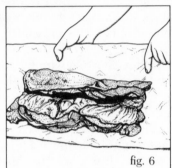

fig. 6

Duck Breast Prosciutto

Duck breasts can be cured as you would pork prosciutto, with salt and air drying. The salt draws out the moisture that would normally spoil the meat during lengthy drying. If you have a cool cellar (below 60°F.), let the breasts air dry there instead of in your refrigerator. Whether air dried or refrigerator aged, begin the recipe at least twelve days before you plan to serve it.

Trim the breasts of overhanging skin and fat leaving a neat skin cap covering the meat. Rub the exposed meat with the garlic. Sprinkle both the meat and skin side with the pepper and salt. Lay the breasts on a plate tilted inside a tray or pan to catch the juices which will be drawn out of the meat. Refrigerate, uncovered, for 2 days.

The breasts from 2 (4-pound) ducks, boned and separated to yield 4 halves
2 Tb. minced garlic
1 Tb. freshly ground black pepper
1 Tb. salt

Rinse the breasts in cold water and pat dry. Using kitchen string, tie the breasts onto a wire rack (such as a cookie or cake cooling rack) so that the air can freely circulate around the meat. Suspend the rack in your refrigerator or tilt upright between shelves and leave uncovered and undisturbed for 10 to 12 days.

When the breasts are ready, they will appear very firm and unbending. (Wrap them individually in plastic wrap and store in the refrigerator for up to one week.)

To serve, slice paper thin slices as you would lox or prosciutto and accompany with fresh fruit or vegetables. You can use duck breast prosciutto in any recipe calling for prosciutto.

Makes 12 servings.

Chicken Salami

*O*ur "salami" is encased in chicken skin. A slice reveals darker chicken and pork meat studded with white chunks of chicken breast, giving the look of salami. Serve with Garlic Mayonnaise.

1 whole (3½-pound)
 chicken, including
 liver
6 ounces pork shoulder
3 slices bacon
2 tsp. minced garlic
1 Tb. chopped fresh
 chives
1½ Tb. marsala or
 sherry
2 tsp. chopped fresh
 thyme
½ tsp. ground nutmeg
¾ tsp. salt
¼ tsp. freshly ground
 black pepper
6 paper thin slices
 prosciutto

Garlic Mayonnaise (see
 page 31)

Preheat oven to 375°F.

Cut off the chicken wings and reserve for another use. Cut the chicken skin down the back with a sharp knife and gently peel the skin off the meat, pulling it down over the legs (fig. 1). Remove it in one piece, being careful not to tear the skin (fig. 2). Lay the skin outer side down on a piece of 12- by 18-inch foil forming a rectangle and set aside.

Remove the breast meat from the chicken. Cut six pencil-width, lengthwise strips; set aside and reserve the rest of the breast meat for another use. Cut the leg and thigh meat from the bones and carefully remove as many white tendons as you can. In a food processor using on-off pulse, or with a sharp knife, chop the leg and thigh meat to hamburger consistency and place in a medium bowl. In the same manner chop the pork, bacon, and chicken liver. Add this to the chopped chicken meat; add the rest of the ingredients except the prosciutto and mayonnaise and mix well.

Cover the chicken skin with the prosciutto slices. Spread the meat mixture over the prosciutto leaving a 1½-inch border on one long side of the skin. Place the breast meat strips randomly on the meat mixture, running lengthwise with the rectangle (fig. 3). On the opposite side of the rectangle from the 1½-inch border, start rolling into a salami shape enclosed in the skin (fig. 4). Roll the foil tightly around the salami twisting the ends closed.

Bake on a cookie sheet for 55 minutes. Let cool in the foil, then refrigerate thoroughly. (It can be stored, refrigerated, for 3 to 4 days.) When ready to serve unwrap the salami and cut into ¼-inch slices. Serve with Garlic Mayonnaise.

Makes 12 servings.

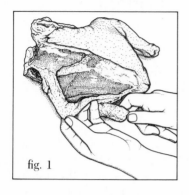

fig. 1

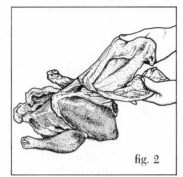

fig. 2

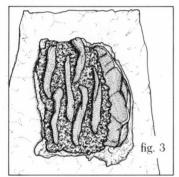

fig. 3

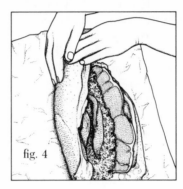

fig. 4

1. Peeling the skin away from the meat.
2. Removing the skin in one piece.
3. Layering the prosciutto, meat mixture and breast meat strips on the skin.
4. Rolling into a salami shape.

Crab with Oregano Marinade

*T*his is a roll-up-your-sleeves type of dish. Your guests have the fun of removing marinated crabmeat from the shell. The light marinade compliments the delicate sweetness of crab. Have small forks, nutcrackers and plenty of napkins on hand.

2 live Dungeness crabs
   (2 to 2½ pounds each)
½ cup lemon juice
1 cup dry white wine
¼ cup fruity olive oil
¼ cup chopped fresh
   oregano leaves (about
   one bunch)
3 scallions, sliced
½ teasoon salt
⅛ tsp. freshly ground
   pepper

In a large pot, bring 1½-inches of water to a boil. Drop in one crab, or two if they will fit, cover, reduce the heat to medium and steam for 10 to 12 minutes. Repeat with the second crab if necessary. Crabs will be bright red when cooked. Cool to room temperature.

To clean the crabs: Pull off and discard the top shell. Turn crab over. Pull off the triangular piece of shell, the "apron," and discard. Turn crab over. Discard the soft gills on either side of the body. Under running water, rinse away any soft insides and pull off any extra bits of shell leaving only the legs and the adjoining body meat.

Using a heavy knife cut the body in half. Twist the claws and legs from the body and cut each body half into several pieces. Using a crab or nut cracker, or the back of a cleaver, crack (do not mash) the leg and claw shells. (The claws, legs and body pieces can be stored, covered and refrigerated, for up to 8 hours.)

Combine the remaining ingredients in a non-aluminum bowl. Let sit, covered and refrigerated, for 1 to 8 hours. To serve, place the crab pieces in the marinade and gently swirl to help the marinade penetrate the cracks in the shell. Let sit 10 minutes. Arrange the crab pieces on a serving plate and drizzle with some of the marinade.

Makes 8 servings.

Flank Steak Dry-marinated with Spices

*T*he far-traveled Romans were well acquainted with sweet spices and pepper. When the empire fell these spices no longer reached Western Europe. It wasn't until after the year 1000 that Venice acquired exclusive trading rights in the Near East and became the dominant spice marketplace in Europe for the next 400 years. Spices were held in such esteem that they served as stable exchange when the value of coins was in doubt. Also, a gift of spices was a valuable bribe to give to an Italian official. Here we use spices to dry-marinate flank steak and contrast their flavors with the bright sweet-sour taste of grapefruit.

Trim steak of excess fat or silvery "skin." In a small bowl combine all of the seasonings. Pat them into the steak, wrap the steak in plastic wrap and marinate in the refrigerator for at least 2 hours or up to 2 days.

One hour before serving, peel the grapefruits of the skin and separate into segments. Remove any white membrane or pith. Dry the segments on a paper towel.

Preheat broiler or grill.

Broil or grill the steak to medium rare. Let the steak cool for 15 minutes. Slice very thinly against the grain. Wrap the grapefruit sections with the steak slices and arrange on a serving plate. Serve at room temperature.

Makes 10 servings.

1 (1¼- to 1½-pound) flank steak
1 tsp. dry mustard
½ tsp. cayenne or red pepper
½ tsp. ground cloves
1 tsp. cinnamon
2 tsp. ground cumin
½ tsp. salt
3 large grapefruits (pink, if available)

Sweet Lamb Sausage Bread

At first glance this looks like a dessert roll but sliced open it reveals a spiral of lamb sausage. As it bakes, the fragrance of the spices permeates the bread. This easy processor-made brioche dough should be started a day in advance.

2 Tb. warm water (105°
  to 115°F)

1 tsp. dry active yeast

2¼ cups (10 ounces)
  bread flour

4½ tsp. sugar

¼ tsp. salt

12 ounces chilled
  butter, cut into ½-
  inch cubes

3 eggs, room
  temperature

¼ cup half and half,
  room temperature

2½ cups Sweet Lamb
  Sausage (page see 92),
  cooked, drained of
  excess fat and cooled

A day ahead:

Warm a small bowl slightly and add the warm water. Stir in the yeast to dissolve it, then mix in 3 tablespoons flour and a pinch of the sugar. Cover the bowl with plastic wrap and let stand in a warm area for 15 minutes. The mixture will be frothy and smell of yeast.

In a food processor with a steel blade, blend the remaining flour, sugar and salt. Add the butter and process for 20 seconds. Add the eggs, half and half, and the yeast mixture. Process without stopping the machine until a soft, sticky dough forms, about 25 seconds. Transfer to a medium buttered bowl and place a piece of plastic wrap loosely on the surface of the dough. Let the dough rise in a warm area until double, 2½ to 3 hours. Stir the dough down, wrap in oiled plastic wrap and chill overnight.

The next day:

On a floured board, roll the dough into a 17- by 12-inch rectangle. If the dough seems to be sticking, loosen it from the board and add more flour. Spread the sausage evenly over the dough leaving a 1½-inch border on one long edge. Start loosely rolling inward from the other long edge in a jellyroll fashion. Tuck the ends of the roll in and place the roll on an oiled cookie sheet, seam side down. Cover with plastic wrap and let rise in a warm area for 2 hours.

Preheat the oven to 350°F.

Uncover dough and bake for 35 minutes or until it is a deep golden color. Cut a slice off of one end of the bread and look at the dough to make sure that it is thoroughly cooked. Cool before cutting. (The sausage bread can be held well-wrapped in plastic at room temperature, for several hours.)

Makes 12 servings.

Prawns in Grappa and Orange

*G*rappa *is Italian white grape brandy. It is a good, all-purpose brandy with a touch of sweetness and more than a touch of unaged sharpness. A charming custom in the Italian Alps is to offer guests a grappa nightcap. We prefer to use grappa in cooking, as in this spicy marinade.*

Peel and devein the prawns, leaving the final segment of shell and tail attached. Combine remaining ingredients, except the olive oil and mustard, in large sauté pan. Bring marinade to a boil, reduce the heat and simmer for 5 minutes. Remove the pan from the heat and whisk in the olive oil and mustard. Add the prawns and simmer (do not boil) over low heat for 1½ minutes. Turn the prawns over and cook for another minute until just underdone. Remove the pan from the heat and let the prawns cool to room temperature in the marinade. (The prawns can be prepared ahead to this point and held, covered at room temperature, for an hour.)

When ready to serve, remove the prawns from the marinade and arrange on a serving plate. Put the extra marinade in a small bowl and serve with the prawns as a dipping sauce.

Makes 8 servings.

1 pound fresh large or jumbo prawns

3 Tb. balsamic vinegar (see page 21)

5 Tb. grappa (or if unavailable light rum or brandy)

¼ cup fresh orange juice

2 tsp. finely chopped orange zest (see page 15)

1 tsp. finely chopped lemon zest (see page 15)

2 Tb. fresh lemon juice

2 Tb. butter

1 Tb. fruity olive oil

1½ tsp. Dijon mustard

Warm and Hot Antipasto Variations

Although these recipes are not traditional to the antipasto table, these warm entrees translate beautifully to the antipasto table adding a hearty dimension that rounds out a selection of antipasti into a meal. Many use traditional Italian ingredients in unusual combinations, such as Sambuca Prawns with Prosciutto. Some are based on classic Italian dishes, for example *Involtini di Vitella* and *Ragu di Tonno*, that are found as a second course in Italy.

Grilled Chard and Fontina Packets

*T**his is a simple antipasto that has had great success at Rapallo. They are trim packets that conceal a center of warm melted cheese and tomatoes.***

8 ounces imported
   Italian fontina

3 or 4 small, ripe but
   firm tomatoes

Salt

Freshly ground black
   pepper

12 large Swiss chard
   leaves, without holes

Light olive oil

Lemon wedges, optional

Cut the cheese into 12 slices, 1½- by 1½-inch by ¼-inch. Cut 12 (¼-inch thick) tomato slices. Lightly salt and pepper the tomatoes.

In a large pot of simmering salted water, blanch the chard leaves a few at a time for 30 seconds. Pat dry and cool. Trim leaves to an approximate 6-inch square, using the discarded edges to patch any holes. Shave the white center rib so that it doesn't protrude too much. Lay the smooth side of the leaves down, place one piece of fontina in the center of each and top with a tomato slice (fig. 1). Fold all sides of the leaf up over the tomato forming a packet (fig. 2). (They can be stored, covered and refrigerated, up to 24 hours before serving.)

Preheat a grill. Brush packets on both sides with olive oil and place on a hot grill, tomato side down. When chard is lightly marked and soft, turn packet with a spatula and grill until the other side is hot. Total cooking time is 3 to 4 minutes. Serve at once with lemon wedges if desired.

Makes 12 servings.

1. Placing the fontina and tomato slices on the center of the chard leaf.
2. Folding chard sides over tomato slice.

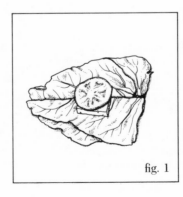

fig. 1

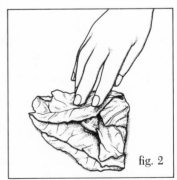

fig. 2

Pasta Fries

*A*t Rapallo, we always have bowls of pasta fries lining the bar. Crunchy and salty, they make a great accompaniment to aperitivi and drinks. Serve them with sandwiches or hamburgers—instead of French fries or potato chips. Made in large batches, pasta fries can be frozen and reheated in minutes in the oven.

In a large pot of rapidly boiling salted water, cook the pasta until tender. Drain the pasta well and toss with a little olive oil to prevent it from sticking.

Heat the vegetable oil in a small saucepan to 350°F or until a small piece of bread starts to bubble a few seconds after being dropped into the oil. Fry just enough pasta to fit comfortably in the pan until it is medium golden brown. Lift the pasta out of the oil with a slotted spoon and drain on paper towels. Repeat until all of the pasta is fried.

If the pasta has stuck together, rub it in between towels to break up the clumps. Put the pasta in a bowl, sprinkle with Parmesan cheese and serve warm or at room temperature.

Makes 7 cups.

1 pound dried imported pasta—our favorites are spirale, gemelli and penne (spirals, helixes and quill shaped)

Light olive oil

Vegetable oil for frying, enough to fill a small saucepan 2 inches deep (approximately 1 quart)

½ cup freshly grated Parmesan cheese

Two-Pesto Polenta Torta

*P*olenta *Torta is so popular that it has become a signature dish of the restaurant. Torta means "cake"; in this case sun-dried tomato and mint pestos between layers of warm polenta. Mint is the favorite herb of the cooks of Rome. It is used as abundantly as parsley and basil are used in other areas of Italy. This dish is ideal for winter because of the year-round availability of mint and sun-dried tomatoes.*

4½ cups water
1 tsp. salt
1¼ cups polenta
½ cup freshly grated Parmesan cheese
4 Tb. butter, room temperature
⅛ tsp. ground white pepper
Light olive oil

3 Tb. Sun-dried Tomato Pesto (recipe follows)
3 Tb. Mint Pesto (recipe follows)

In a large heavy saucepan bring the water to a boil. Add the salt and reduce the heat to a slow boil. Constantly stirring in one direction add the polenta in a slow, steady stream. Continue stirring until the polenta starts to thicken. Reduce the heat to the lowest level possible and cook, stirring often, for 40 minutes.

Remove the polenta from the heat and beat in the Parmesan, butter and white pepper. Spread the polenta onto a lightly oiled cookie sheet, into a rectangle 12- by 13- by ½-inch thick. Cool to room temperature, cover with plastic wrap and refrigerate for at least one hour.

Cut the polenta into eighteen 2½-inch circles. (They can be stored, wrapped and refrigerated, for several days.)

Preheat broiler.

Place the polenta circles on a lightly oiled cookie sheet and place in broiler until they are hot, about 2 minutes. Assemble the torta by topping 6 of the circles with 1½ teaspoons sun-dried pesto each, spreading it to within ¼-inch of the edge of the circles. Top these with another circle and spread with the mint pesto, leaving a ¼-inch edge. Top with the remaining 6 circles to form 6 torta, 3 polenta layers tall. We like to garnish the top of the torta with a few strips of sun-dried tomato. Serve at once.

Makes 6 servings.

MINT PESTO

Chop the mint, parsley, pine nuts, garlic, salt and olive oil in a food processor or blender on high speed. Stop the machine occasionally to scrape down the sides. Process to a fairly smooth puree.

Pour the pesto into a small bowl and beat in the room temperature butter. Place a piece of plastic directly on the surface until you are ready to use it. (Pesto can be stored, covered and refrigerated, for up to 4 days.)

Makes ½ cup.

1¼ cups loosely packed fresh mint leaves
6 Tb. loosely packed fresh parsley leaves
1 Tb. pine nuts, lightly toasted
¾ tsp. finely chopped garlic
¼ tsp. salt
¼ cup light olive oil
1½ Tb. butter, room temperature

SUN-DRIED TOMATO PESTO

Add all of the ingredients to a food processor and run for 15 seconds, scraping the side once. The mixture should be finely chopped but not pureed. (The pesto can be stored, covered and refrigerated, for up to a week.)

Makes ½ cup.

2 tsp. chopped garlic
12 sun-dried tomatoes
1½ Tb. olive oil from the sun-dried tomatoes
2 Tb. pine nuts, lightly toasted
3 Tb. chopped parsley

Arborio Rice Frittata

*F**rittata is a thick, slow-cooked Italian omelette that can be made with various savory ingredients. We like to choose ingredients that add a textural contrast to the eggs. In this recipe we use arborio rice which keeps its distinctively chewy texture and rich taste whether served hot or room temperature.*

2 extra large artichokes
2 cups water
1 tsp. salt
1 cup arborio rice (see page 11)
6 ounces pancetta (see page 18)
3 Tb. light olive oil
2 ounces provolone cheese, cut into ¼-inch dice
½ cup freshly grated Parmesan cheese
Pinch freshly ground black pepper
1 Tb. chopped fresh sage
8 eggs, lightly beaten

Steam or boil the artichokes until tender. Peel off all of the leaves and the choke; trim the very end of the stem and discard. Slice the remaining bottom and stem into thin slices and set aside.

In a medium saucepan, bring the water to a boil. Add the salt and rice, then lower the heat to a simmer. Cover tightly and cook until the rice is tender, about 20 minutes.

Meanwhile chop the pancetta into ½-inch cubes. Fry the pancetta over medium-high heat in 1 tablespoon of the olive oil. When evenly brown, drain the pancetta on a paper towel and reserve 2 tablespoons of the fat.

In a large bowl combine the rice, pancetta, artichoke slices, cheeses, pepper, sage and the reserved 2 tablespoons of pancetta oil. Cool to room temperature. (Mixture can be prepared ahead, covered and refrigerated, for up to 8 hours.)

Preheat broiler.

Heat a 9-inch sauté pan over medium-high heat. Stir the eggs into the rice mixture. Add 1 tablespoon of the olive oil to the pan and half (2¼ cups) of the rice mixture. Cook over medium heat until the frittata is heated through and firm, about 6 minutes. Place the frittata under the broiler to set and lightly brown the top.

Transfer the frittata to a plate and cover loosely with foil to keep warm while you cook the remaining rice mixture. Cut the frittatas into wedges and serve at once or at room temperature.

Makes 8 servings.

Garlic Bread Custards

This is a soufflé-like pudding that is a great way to use day-old bread. Although the recipe seems to call for a lot of garlic, a mild flavor results from the long cooking.

Preheat the oven to 350°F.

Use 2 tablespoons of butter to grease 8 straight-sided baking cups (or a 1½-quart soufflé dish).

Place the bread and the butter pieces in a large bowl. In a small saucepan, bring the milk to just below boiling and pour all but 2 tablespoons over the bread. Do not stir; set aside for at least 30 minutes while the milk soaks into the bread.

In a small bowl, combine the egg yolks, garlic, Parmesan, salt and the remaining 2 tablespoons of milk. Gently fold this mixture into the soaked bread.

Whip the egg whites to soft, not dry peaks and fold them into the bread mixture. Divide the custard equally among the cups and bake for about 50 minutes (1 hour, 5 minutes in a soufflé dish), or until the custard is puffed, golden brown, and set in the center. Cool for 15 minutes (they will fall as they cool) and unmold.

Place the custards on a serving plate and surround them with the slices of prosciutto.

Makes 8 servings.

2 Tb. butter, room temperature
2½ cups (1-inch) cubes of crustless bread
¼ cup butter, cut into small pieces
2 cups milk
6 eggs, separated
2 Tb. finely chopped garlic
½ cup finely grated Parmesan cheese
½ tsp. salt
24 paper-thin slices prosciutto

Onion and Anchovy Tart

*T*his tart has a distinctly Sicilian flair. Onions are slowly cooked to give them a rich sweet flavor and are combined with anchovies, olives and raisins. Pasta Frolla is a basic Italian tart dough and is easy to work with. The shell and filling can both be made ahead and assembled just before serving.

2 Tb. light olive oil

5 cups thinly sliced yellow onions

1 cup coarsley chopped calamata olives (or other good quality black olives)

7 anchovy fillets, rinsed and mashed

3 medium tomatoes, peeled, seeded and chopped

⅓ cup golden raisins

⅓ cup black raisins

6 ounces cream cheese

1 baked 9-inch Pasta Frolla pastry shell or 4 4-inch individual pastry shells (recipe follows)

Heat a large heavy sauté pan over medium heat until hot. Add the olive oil and onions. Sauté until the onions are golden, 20 to 25 minutes. Add the olives, anchovies, tomatoes and raisins. Reduce the heat to medium low and let the mixture cook for 30 to 40 minutes, stirring occasionally. When done the mixture should appear dry. (The onion mixture can be prepared ahead to this point and stored, covered and refrigerated, for up to one week.)

Preheat oven to 400°F.

Spread the cream cheese on the bottom of the pastry shell(s). Heat the shell(s) in the oven until the cheese is warm, about 5 minutes. Meanwhile, heat the onion mixture in a sauté pan over medium heat. When the mixture is hot, pour it into the warmed pastry shells(s). Cut the large shell into 8 pieces, the small shells in half and serve.

Makes 8 servings.

PASTA FROLLA

2½ cups all-purpose flour

¼ tsp. salt (if using unsalted butter)

8 ounces chilled butter, cut into ½-inch cubes

4 to 6 Tb. ice water

In a large bowl, place the flour and salt, if needed. Add the butter and combine with your finger tips until the butter is the size of peas. Gradually add the water, stirring with a fork until the dough holds together. Gather the dough into a ball, wrap well with plastic wrap and refrigerate for at least one hour (or up to 3 days).

Let the dough soften at room temperature until it can be rolled. Roll the dough ⅛-inch thick and 3 inches wider than the tart pan. Gently lift the dough into the pan and press the dough down into the corners. Trim the excess dough and pinch the edge decoratively. The scraps can be rerolled or frozen for later use. Chill for 15 minutes, wrapped in plastic wrap. (The shell can be prepared ahead to this point and stored, covered and refrigerated, for up to 2 days or frozen for 2 weeks.)

Preheat the oven to 375°F.

Line the crust with foil and fill it with dried beans to weight it down. Bake for 20 minutes, remove the beans and the foil and continue baking until the crust is nicely brown, 15 to 20 minutes. If using a frozen shell, bake it without thawing, adding 5 to 10 minutes to the cooking time. Cool the shell before using.

Makes one 9-inch or 10-inch shell.

Mozzarella and Pepper Spiedini
Skewered Mozzarella and Peppers

S *piedini means "skewer" and Italians will skewer almost any food: meats, fish, cheese, bread. Spiedini alla Romana is the famous dish of mozzarella and bread with anchovies and olive oil. Our colorful spiedini combines onions, peppers, mozzarella and garlic and is fun to eat right off of the skewer. If you have long fresh rosemary twigs, strip off the leaves except for a tassle at the end and use it as your skewer.*

MARINADE

1 cup Chianti or other full-bodied wine

½ cup red wine vinegar

1 tsp. sugar

½ tsp. salt

¼ tsp. freshly ground black pepper

1 medium red onion, peeled and cut into quarters

2 red or yellow bell peppers, roasted and peeled (see page 12)

6 ounces mozzarella cheese (see page 14)

Salt

Freshly ground black pepper

12 1-inch cubes of crustless day-old Italian or French white bread

¼ cup fruity olive oil

In a small saucepan combine the marinade ingredients. Heat the marinade until it is too hot to touch and remove from heat. Separate the onion quarters into individual layers, drop them into the marinade and set aside for at least 30 minutes.

Cut the peppers lengthwise into twelve 1-inch wide strips. Cut the mozzarella into twelve 1-inch cubes. Sprinkle the cheese with salt and pepper and wrap each with a pepper strip. On bamboo or metal skewers alternate the wrapped mozzarella, bread cubes and pieces of marinated onion. Place skewers on a lightly oiled cookie sheet until ready to serve.

Preheat broiler.

Broil the skewered cheese and vegetables on the cookie sheet until the cheese begins to melt, then turn the skewer over. When the cheese begins to run again remove the skewers to a heated serving plate, drizzle with olive oil and serve at once.

Makes 8 servings.

Amalfi-style Sandwiches

These sandwiches are a variation of ones we have eaten along the Amalfi coast in Italy where they fry a light spongy bread around mozzarella cheese. When first developing this recipe we tried to use a variety of excellent fresh bakery-made breads: peasant-style, sourdough, Tuscan, potato, etc.—and all failed. We found that the only bread that worked was the soft, supermarket bread of our childhood. (Remember mashing a slice into a little hard ball as a child?) Only this soft, spongy bread can be squashed enough to make a tight seal and not rip, causing leakage. The result is the appropriate light covering for this tangy filling.

16 slices (about a 1-pound loaf) white bread

4 ounces bel paese cheese

3 Tb. coarsely chopped Pickled Pepper (see page 26)

1 Tb. finely chopped stemmed pepperoncini (see COOK'S NOTE)

1 Tb. finely chopped anchovy

Vegetable oil for frying, enough to fill a large saucepan 2-inches deep, about 1½ quarts

1 cup all-purpose flour

2 eggs, lightly beaten

¼ cup milk

Cut the crusts from the bread slices. Cut the bel paese into 8 slices about 1½ inches square, or press together smaller pieces. Top 8 of the bread slices with a slice of bel paese and sprinkle each with the peppers, pepperoncini and anchovy. Top with the remaining bread slices.

Quickly dip the edges of the sandwiches into a bowl of water. Squash the edges together with your fingertips to make a tight seal—the edges will be soggy and mashed. (At this point the sandwiches can be stored, covered and refrigerated, for several hours before serving.)

Heat the vegetable oil to 375°F. or until a piece of bread crust bubbles immediately after being dropped into the oil. Put the flour in a bowl, combine the eggs with the milk in another. Check the edges of the sandwiches to make sure that they are well sealed. Dip each sandwich into the flour to coat and shake off excess. Submerge in the egg mixture to coat thoroughly and let the excess drip off. Coat again lightly in the flour. Fry the sandwiches 2 or 3 at a time, turning them once. Remove them when they are golden brown, about 6 minutes. Drain the sandwiches on a paper towel for 5 minutes before serving.

Makes 8 sandwiches.

COOK'S NOTE

Pepperoncini, also known as Golden Greek peppers, are small golden-green pickled peppers. They are found in most supermarkets and delicatessans. Buy imported brands.

Sfincione
Sicilian-style Pizza

In Palermo each bakery, snack shop and street cart sells its own version of sfincione. It ranges from tiny pizzas with a variety of toppings to thick, square slabs of bread simply drizzled with olive oil. More delicate versions use potato in the dough which gives it a moist yet crisp texture. We form our irregularly shaped sfincione small enough to be easily held in the hand.

1 large potato, baked
1½ tsp. dry yeast
½ cup lukewarm water (95° to 100°F.)
2½ cups all-purpose flour
½ tsp. salt
½ cup lukewarm milk (95° to 100°F.)
1 Tb. fruity olive oil
Flour
Light olive oil

Peel the potato and put through a ricer or a sieve. Set aside ½ cup plus 2 tablespoons. Save the rest for another use. (We always end up eating it while preparing the rest of the recipe.)

In a small bowl sprinkle the yeast over the water. Let sit in a warm draft-free place for 5 minutes or until the yeast is dissolved. Stir to combine.

In a large ceramic or glass bowl combine the potato, flour and salt. Form a well in the center and add the yeast mixture, milk and fruity olive oil. Blend to form a soft dough. On a lightly floured surface knead the dough, folding it towards you and pushing it away, until the dough is smooth and elastic, 10 to 15 minutes. Flour the surface lightly as needed to prevent sticking. Gather the dough into a ball, lightly rub it with olive oil and place it in a large bowl. Let rise, covered with a towel, in a warm draft-free place, such as an oven with a pilot light, for 1½ to 2 hours or until double. Punch the dough down. (The dough can be covered with plastic wrap and refrigerated overnight.)

For each sfincione pull off a 1-ounce piece of dough, about the size of a golfball, and flatten slightly between your palms into a disc. Use your fingertips to hold the disc in the air, stretching it in all directions to widen the round into a 4-inch circle. Lightly flour your hands if there is any sticking. The center should be thin enough to see light through and the edges should have a ¼-inch thick rim. Place the round on a lightly oiled cookie sheet. When all rounds are formed, cover the cookie sheet with a towel and set it in a warm place to rise until the edges are double.

Preheat oven to 425°F.

Bake the rounds on the floor of the oven for 7 to 10 minutes or until the bottoms are brown. The top should be pale. (At this point sfincione can be cooled, wrapped and refrigerated for 24 hours or frozen for up to 1 week.)

Preheat oven to 375°F.

Place the sfincione on a cookie sheet and top with desired ingredients (see COOK'S NOTE). If they are frozen it is not necessary to thaw them. Bake in the top third of the oven until toppings are hot and the crust is brown, 7 to 10 minutes. Brush the crust with a little olive oil and serve at once.

Makes 14 to 16 rounds.

COOK'S NOTE

Choose a moist sauce or juicy vegetable: your favorite tomato sauce, (such as Suppli Sauce page 33), fresh tomato slices, fried slices of green tomato or roasted peppers, for example. Top this with one or two other ingredients: cheeses, fresh herbs, bitter greens, olives, fried onions, raw peppers, capers, baked or pickled garlic.

Garlic Crespelle with Bel Paese

Crespelle (thin pancakes or crepes) are used throughout Italy to wrap anything from meats and fish to cheeses and sweets. Here they are spread with baked garlic and topped with melted bel paese.

3 eggs
⅔ cup milk
⅔ cup water
¼ tsp. salt
3 Tb. garlic oil (see page 16)
1 cup all-purpose flour
1 tsp. vegetable oil
2 heads (3 Tb.) Baked Garlic, peeled and smashed into a paste (recipe follows)
10 ounces bel paese cheese
¾ cup Onion Marmellata (see page 42)

Put the eggs, milk, water, salt and garlic oil in a food processor. Process for 5 seconds. Add half of the flour and process for 5 seconds. Scrape down the side and add the remaining flour and process for 5 seconds. Pour into a bowl, cover and refrigerate for at least 1 hour for the batter to become more tender.

Heat an 8-inch non-stick sauté or omelette pan over medium-high heat until hot. Reduce the heat to medium. Coat the pan lightly with 1 teaspoon vegetable oil and wipe out extra with a paper towel leaving only a thin film. Pour 2 tablespoons of batter into the hot pan. Quickly swirl the pan to distribute the batter in an even, thin layer covering the bottom of the pan. Cook until the bottom turns light brown, 15 to 30 seconds, and with a rubber spatula loosen the edge of the crepe and flip it over. Cook for 10 seconds and remove to a cookie sheet to cool. Do not stack the crepes or they will stick. Continue until all of the batter is used.

The cooled crepes can be stacked with a piece of wax paper or plastic wrap between each one. (Well wrapped in plastic and refrigerated, they can be stored 2 to 3 days.)

Preheat broiler.

Spread a scant teaspoon of baked garlic paste on the least attractive side of 12 of the crepes making a thin, even coating. (Freeze remaining crepes for later use.) Loosely fold each crepe into quarters to form a rustic looking triangle. Place the crepes on a ovenproof serving tray with at least 1 inch around each crepe.

Cut the bel paese into 12 triangles that are approximately the same size as the folded crepes and ¼ inch thick. Place one piece of bel paese on each folded crepe. Place under the broiler and cook until the cheese starts to bubble, 2 to 4 minutes. Serve at once with Onion Marmellata.

Makes 12 servings.

BAKED GARLIC

Preheat oven to 300°F.

    With a small sharp knife, trim off the stem and the top ¼ inch of the head, exposing a few of the cloves. Peel off the papery outer skins without detaching any cloves. Arrange the heads in an ovenproof dish and pour the oil over them. Bake, covered, for ½ hour. Remove the cover and continue to bake until the garlic is golden brown, very soft, and sweet, one hour or more.

    Cool to room temperature and peel gently (see COOK'S NOTE). (Store in a well sealed container in the refrigerator for up to 2 weeks.)

    Makes ½ cup puree of 4 individual heads.

4 whole heads garlic
(firm and not
sprouting)
½ cup fruity olive oil

COOK'S NOTE

It is easier to peel the cloves before refrigeration. If you want to serve the heads whole, pour an additional ¼ cup of light olive oil over them, sprinkle with ½ teaspoon salt and ¼ teaspoon freshly ground black pepper. Store covered at room temperature for up to 12 hours before serving.

Crostini

C rostini, small toasts with a variety of toppings, are a traditional antipasto using day-old bread. They can be served hot or room temperature (see page 52 for room temperature recipes). We like to serve some of each at a gathering. Toast the bread ahead, then top and heat just before serving.

TOPPINGS

- **Marinated Mozzarella, page 31**
- **Onion Marmellata , page 42**
- **Baked Garlic, page 83**
- **Various cheeses (mozzarella, bel paese, fontina, etc.) topped with roasted peppers or sliced fresh tomatoes**

Make Crostini according to recipe on page 52.

Top the crostini with any of the toppings and place under a preheated broiler for 1 to 2 minutes until the toppings are hot or the cheese starts to melt.

Fish Spiedini with Pickled Garlic
Skewered Fish

Garlic, so strongly identified with Italian cooking, is used extensively in Asian cuisines, often as a pickle. We have taken this idea and made it a little more Italian, using balsamic vinegar and olive oil. Pickled garlic can also be used as a condiment for grilled meats or poultry.

Cut the fish into 1-inch cubes and place on wooden or metal skewers. Brush with olive oil and sprinkle with salt and pepper. On a hot grill or a preheated broiler, cook the fish turning the skewers so that each side cooks evenly. The cooking time will vary with each fish but will be only a few minutes. The fish should still have a blush of pink inside or in the case of tuna a medium red color.

Arrange the skewers on a plate and baste with a little of the Pickled Garlic liquid. Sprinkle the garlic over the fish or, as we like to do, serve it to the side cupped in a radicchio leaf.

Makes 12 servings.

1½ pounds skinless fish fillets (choose a firm-fleshed variety such as swordfish, angler, redfish, tuna or sturgeon)
Light olive oil
Salt
Freshly ground black pepper
Pickled Garlic (recipe follows)

PICKLED GARLIC

In a small saucepan over medium heat, bring all of the ingredients except the oil to a simmer and cook until the garlic is tender but not mushy, about 45 minutes. If necessary add a few tablespoons of water during cooking to keep the garlic cloves covered.

With a slotted spoon remove the garlic to cool and discard the bay leaf. Boil the liquid until reduced to 2 tablespoons. Combine the liquid and the olive oil in a small storage jar. Slice the garlic cloves thinly and add them to the jar. (Keep the garlic tightly sealed in the refrigerator; it will last for several weeks.)

Makes ½ cup sliced cloves.

20 whole garlic cloves, peeled
1 cup red wine
1 Tb. soy sauce
3 Tb. balsamic vinegar
1 Tb. sugar
1 bay leaf
2 Tb. fruity olive oil

Calamari with Balsamic Marinade

*T*he secret to tender calamari is a very brief cooking time. The moment it turns from translucent to opaque and the edges begin to curl it is done. Instructions are given for grilling but the calamari can also be broiled in the same manner. By sprinkling the cooked calamari with the marinade, it will have a handsome, brown sheen.

4 one-inch sprigs rosemary, bruised

1 cup balsamic vinegar (see page 21)

1 Tb. sugar

1 cup chianti or other dry red wine

1 tsp. finely chopped garlic

¼ cup fruity olive oil

1 pound cleaned calamari or 2 pounds uncleaned

In a medium bowl combine all ingredients except the calamari. Let sit at room temperature for at least one hour.

Meanwhile, clean the calamari by cutting off the tentacles just above the eyes. Remove and discard the hard ball in the base of the tentacles. Cut one side of the body open lengthwise so that it lies flat in one piece. Remove all innards and the plastic-like quill backbone by scraping with the back of a knife. Rinse the body sac and tentacles very well. (Calamari can be done ahead to this point and refrigerated, covered, for up to 8 hours.) Add the calamari to the marinade and let sit for 10 to 15 minutes.

Preheat grill.

Remove the tentacles from the marinade, place on the grill and cook for 2 minutes, turning once. Transfer to a warm plate. Place some of the calamari sacs on the grill and cook for 1 minute, turning once. Place on the warm plate. Continue until all the sacs are grilled. Spoon some of the marinade over the top of the squid and serve at once.

Makes 8 servings.

Tonno Ripiene
Stuffed Tuna

S *lices of tuna are stuffed (ripiene) with a bold mixture of piquant ingredients: sun-dried tomatoes, green olives, red onions. To us these are the tastes of the Mediterranean.*

In a medium bowl mix all the filling ingredients. Taste for salt as sun-dried tomatoes vary greatly in saltiness. Set this filling aside, covered, for one hour for the bread crumbs to absorb the flavor.

Slice the fish into ¼-inch thick slices, 2 to 3 inches across. If they are longer cut them into 2 pieces. Between sheets of wax paper pound the fish gently with your fist to flatten them until they are ⅛-inch thick. When all the pieces are flattened, divide the filling evenly among them, placing it in the center of each piece. Fold the pieces in half covering the filling in a turnover fashion. (Ripiene can be prepared ahead to this point, covered with plastic wrap and refrigerated for up to 12 hours.)

Preheat a grill or broiler.

Brush the tuna packets with olive oil, sprinkle with salt and pepper and cook for a few minutes on each side until firm but still pink inside. Remove to a serving plate and serve at once, garnished with lemon slices.

Makes 12 servings.

FILLING

⅔ cup finely chopped sun-dried tomatoes, packed in oil (see page 20)

½ cup finely chopped green olives

2 Tb. minced red onion

2 Tb. minced red pepper

1 cup fine bread crumbs

2 Tb. olive oil from the sun-dried tomatoes

1 Tb. fresh lemon juice

Salt to taste

2 pounds fresh tuna fillet, skinless

Fruity olive oil

Freshly ground black pepper

Lemon slices for garnish

Ragu di Tonno
Tuna Ragout

*T*his tuna "stew" is from Western Sicily, where the city of Trapani has made tuna its livelihood since Greek times. This ragout can be served with polenta or rice, but is especially good served over couscous in the Arab-Sicilian style particular to Trapani.

SAUCE
1 Tb. light olive oil
2 cups sliced red onion
¾ cup white wine
1 (28-ounce) can diced Italian tomatoes, undrained, or 2 cups diced fresh tomatoes, peeled, cored and seeded (about 4 medium tomatoes)
1½ tsp. chopped fresh mint
1½ cups clam juice
¼ tsp. salt
Freshly ground black pepper

1½ pounds fresh tuna, cut into 1-inch cubes
3 Tb. flour
Salt
Freshly ground black pepper
2 Tb. light olive oil

In a medium saucepan, heat 1 tablespoon of olive oil. Add the onions and cook over low heat until soft but not brown, 8 to 10 minutes. Add the white wine, tomatoes and mint. Cook over low heat until reduced to ½ cup of liquid, 15 to 20 minutes. Add the clam juice, salt and pepper. Bring to a boil, then simmer for 20 to 25 minutes or until reduced by half. (The sauce can be prepared ahead and stored, covered and refrigerated, for up to three days.)

Dust the tuna lightly with flour, shake off the excess, and sprinkle with salt and pepper. In a sauté pan large enough to hold the tuna in a single layer, heat the 2 tablespoons of olive oil. Add the tuna and cook over medium heat, turning occasionally, until just lightly colored on all sides, 3 to 4 minutes. Add the tomato-onion sauce and simmer until the tuna is done but still pink inside, 4 to 5 minutes. Serve at once.

Makes 8 servings.

Bacon-wrapped Fennel

*T*his irresistible fall and winter dish uses one of the most loved vegetables in Italy—fennel. Fresh fennel bulbs are available October through March. The slight licorice taste is well matched to the smoky bacon. Present these wrapped spears on a bed of the fennel tops.

Cut the fennel bulbs in half lengthwise. Cut the halves lengthwise into wedges that are 1-inch wide, leaving part of the core in the base to keep the wedge together.

Place the fennel wedges in a large sauté pan and cover with the chicken stock. Cover the pan and simmer, turning once, until they are crisp-tender. Remove the fennel and save the stock for other uses, such as vegetable soup.

Preheat broiler or grill.

Wrap each wedge with a slice of bacon and secure with a toothpick if necessary. (The wedges can be prepared ahead to this point, covered and refrigerated for up to 4 hours.)

Place the wedges on a hot grill or a broiler pan. Cook, turning once, until the bacon becomes crisp, about 3 minutes on each side. Arrange the wedges on a warmed serving plate covered with fennel tops. Grind fresh black pepper over the wedges just before serving.

Makes 12 servings.

1 pound trimmed fresh fennel bulb (see COOK's NOTE)
1 cup chicken stock
8 ounces bacon (12 slices)
Freshly ground black pepper

COOK'S NOTE

Fennel bulbs, also known as sweet anise, often come with the stalks and feathery leaves attached. To trim fennel, remove the stalks, leaves and the outside layer of the bulb if it seems tough and discolored. Keep the leaves for garnish.

Involtini di Vitella
Grilled Veal Rolls

*I*nspiration for this dish comes from Lo Scudiero restaurant *in Palermo, Sicily. The highlight of a memorable lunch of great dishes was the grilled veal rolls stuffed with ground salami and herbs. It is an unusual treatment of veal that is perfect for the antipasto table.*

⅓ cup freshly grated
Parmesan cheese

1 egg

½ cup coarsely chopped
red bell pepper

¼ cup fresh marjoram
or oregano

6 cloves Baked Garlic
(see page 83)

½ cup coarsely chopped
red onion

4 ounces mortadella

5 ounces dry salami,
rind removed

16 slices (about 1 pound)
pounded veal
scallopini (see
COOK'S NOTE)

In a medium bowl combine the Parmesan and the egg. On a large work surface chop the pepper, marjoram or oregano, garlic, onion, mortadella and salami to a fine mince. Add this to the cheese-egg mixture and mix well.

Divide the stuffing evenly among the veal slices using about 2 tablespoons per slice. Roll each slice into a cigar shape. (The veal can be prepared to this point and stored, covered and refrigerated, for up to 8 hours.)

Preheat broiler or grill.

Oil a hot grill or broiler pan and put the rolls on it seam side down. Turn them gently once while cooking. They are done when the pink has just disappeared from the center and they feel firm to the touch. Serve at once on a heated plate.

Makes 8 servings.

COOK'S NOTE

This method also works well with pork loin. Use 2 pounds of boneless pork loin, trimmed and cut into ½-inch slices. Butterfly the slices and pound them ⅛-inch thick. Stuff and cook using the procedures in this recipe.

Onions Filled with Sweet Lamb Sausage

P *lain, whole baked onions are often seen on antipasto tables. Sausage-stuffed onions are a hearty and interesting variation. The juices from the sausage combine with olive oil and balsamic vinegar to permeate the onion. We love the exotic flair given by the sweet lamb sausage, but you can also use your favorite sausage recipe.*

Preheat the oven to 350°F.

Shave ⅛ inch off the top and bottom of each onion. Using a melon baller or a small, sharp knife, carve out the interior of each onion, forming a pocket, without breaking through the bottom of the onion. Stuff each onion to overflowing using about ¼ cup of sausage meat per onion.

Set the onions in a small ovenproof pan just large enough to hold them. Combine the oil and vinegar and pour over the onions. Sprinkle with the salt and pepper. Add the water to the pan without pouring it over the onions. (This dish can be prepared ahead to this point and stored, covered and refrigerated, overnight.) Cover tightly and bake for 1 hour and 15 minutes, or until the onions are tender throughout.

Cool onions for 15 minutes then cut in half or into wedge-shaped quarters. Arrange on a serving plate and baste with the pan juices. They can also be served room temperature.

Makes 8 servings.

4 large yellow onions, peeled
1 cup Sweet Lamb Sausage (recipe follows)
2 Tb. fruity olive oil
2 Tb. balsamic vinegar
1 tsp. salt
¼ tsp. freshly ground black pepper
½ cup water

COOK'S NOTE

Fat back is ideal for making the sausage, but if it is impossible to locate, substitute the same quantity of salt pork. Dice the salt pork into ½-inch cubes and drop into boiling water. Remove the pot from the heat and let rest for 5 minutes. Drain the salt pork cubes and chill thoroughly before grinding. If using salt pork, use only 1 teaspoon of salt instead of 2 and taste for seasoning.

Sweet Lamb Sausage

With almonds, currants and sweet spices, this sausage reflects the Arabic influence on Southern Italian cooking. The pomegranate juice lends a piquant sweetness that heightens the lamb flavor and gives it an intriguing taste.

1 pound boned lamb shoulder (or stew meat)

½ cup diced onion

5 cloves garlic, peeled and smashed

1 scallion, chopped

1 cup pomegranate juice (available at health food stores)

4 Tb. red wine

2 Tb. fruity olive oil

4 ounces pork shoulder (or stew meat), cut into 1-inch cubes and chilled

5 ounces pork fat back, (see COOK'S NOTE, page 91), cut into ½-inch cubes and chilled

2 tsp. whole cumin seeds

¼ tsp. ground cloves

1 tsp. ground cinnamon

1 tsp. cayenne pepper

¾ tsp. nutmeg

2 tsp. salt

1 Tb. marsala or cream sherry

2 Tb. currants

2 Tb. slivered almonds, toasted

Trim the lamb of sinews, cut into 1-inch cubes and combine in a bowl with the onion, garlic, scallion, ½ cup pomegranate juice, 2 tablespoons red wine and the olive oil. Cover well and refrigerate overnight.

Remove the lamb, onion, garlic and scallion from the marinade, discard the liquid, and return the lamb mixture to the refrigerator. Chill your meat grinder parts or food processor work bowl and steel blade in the freezer for 15 minutes. Working quickly to retain the cold temperature, grind the lamb and the vegetables to a medium grind. If using a food processor, chop the meat first, 1 cup at a time, using 4 or 5 two-second pulses until the meat is a medium grind but holds together. Next process the vegetables to the same grind. Set aside in a large bowl. Remove and discard any large pieces of sinew or gristle.

Grind the pork shoulder and fat back (making sure that they are well chilled) as you did with the lamb and add to the bowl. Add the seasonings, the remaining 2 tablespoons red wine and marsala, and toss mixture lightly; do not overmix.

In a small saucepan over medium heat, boil the remaining ½ cup pomegranate juice until reduced to 2 tablespoons and set aside. When cool add the juice, the currants and almonds to the meat mixture and toss lightly. Fry 1 tablespoon of the mixture in oil, taste and adjust seasoning, if necessary. Refrigerate sausage until needed.

(The sausage can be stored, covered and refrigerated, for up to one week. It also freezes very well. Once thawed, gently remix the exuded liquids back into the meat.)

Makes 3½ cups.

Sambuca Prawns with Prosciutto

Many Mediterranean countries have anise-flavored liquores; Italy has Sambuca. Manufactured by hundreds of producers, it is commonly served throughout the country as an after dinner drink. Sambuca gives these simple grilled prawns a surprising complexity.

Peel and devein the prawns leaving the final segment of shell and tail attached. Place the prawns in a small bowl with the Sambuca and the fruity olive oil. Marinate the prawns, covered, in the refrigerator, for at least 30 minutes but no longer than 1 hour, tossing occasionally.

Cut the prosciutto slices in half lengthwise. Drain each prawn, sprinkle with pepper and wrap with a slice of prosciutto. (They can be prepared ahead to this point, covered and refrigerated for 2 to 3 hours.)

Preheat a grill or broiler.

Brush the prosciutto and prawns with the light olive oil and grill or broil them, turning once, until the prosciutto starts to crisp and the prawns lose their translucent look and turn opaque throughout, about 4 minutes.

While hot, place the prawns on a serving plate accompanied by lemon wedges.

Makes 8 servings.

1 pound large fresh prawns
½ cup Sambuca Liquore
½ cup fruity olive oil
8 to 10 paper-thin slices prosciutto
1 tsp. freshly ground black pepper
¼ cup light olive oil
Lemon wedges, for garnish

Dolci

The most common dolci, or desserts, in Italy are fresh fruits; they follow nearly every meal in the home. Restaurants offer light desserts such as strawberries with balsamic vinegar and zabaglione. Dolci also are sweets eaten in cafes with a midday espresso or ices such as granita eaten as a summer refresher.

The recipes in this chapter are uncomplicated, both in ingredients and preparation. They provide a sweet note that rounds out a meal of many tastes and textures.

Dates and Ricotta

For thousands of years dates have been one of the most important foods in the Middle East and the Mediterranean. They can have up to an astonishing 60% sugar. Although dates are eaten fresh in producing countries, we see them in a semi-dry state. Look for dates that feel soft and moist to the touch, not firm and dry.

8 ounces pitted dates
½ cup ricotta cheese
2 pinches ground cloves
¼ tsp. ground nutmeg
½ tsp. poppy seeds
½ tsp. sugar
¼ cup sliced almonds, toasted

Slice the dates lengthwise on one side and gently open without separating the halves. Mix together the ricotta, cloves, nutmeg, poppy seeds and sugar. Fill each date with ¾ teaspoon stuffing. Slightly close the halves and leave some ricotta showing. Press a few almond slices into the ricotta on each date. Arrange on a serving tray. (Dates can be stuffed several hours ahead and stored, covered and refrigerated.)
Makes 8 servings.

Oranges with Amontillado Sherry

Sometimes the finest combinations are the simplest. Amontillado sherry, with its rich, nutty flavor is perfect with oranges. The almonds add a nice textural contrast. The combined orange juice and sherry left in the bottom of the bowl is a delicious ending.

9 medium navel oranges
1 cup plus 2 Tb. Amontillado sherry
¾ cup sliced almonds, toasted

With a sharp knife, peel the oranges so that no white pith remains. Cut in half lengthwise, then slice crosswise into ½-inch thick half moons. Put orange slices in a large glass bowl, pour the sherry over and top with almonds. Garnish with sprigs of fresh mint.
Makes 8 servings.

Apricots with Biscotti and Pine Nut Filling

*I*talian *biscotti and cookies are made with almonds, fennel seeds, lemon and other flavorful ingredients which give the stuffing a distinctive taste. They can be found in Italian delicatessans and specialty markets.*

Cut the apricots in half, discard the pits and set aside. In a small bowl combine the pine nuts, biscotti and vermouth. Sprinkle the cut side of each apricot half lightly with sugar. Put a heaping teaspoon of filling in each apricot half. (Apricots can be stuffed up to an hour before serving.)

Makes 4 servings.

4 ripe apricots
2 Tb. coarsely chopped pine nuts, toasted
¼ cup coarsley chopped biscotti, or any other crisp, dry Italian cookie, such as amaretti
2 Tb. bianco vermouth
½ tsp. superfine sugar

Mascarpone Rolled in Hazelnuts

*M*ascarpone, *a thick, clotted cream traditionally from Lodi in Piedmont, is imported to this country and available in Italian food stores and most cheese shops. It's worth requesting as there is no substitute. Frangelico is a rich, smooth liquore made in Italy from hazelnuts. The combination is a very elegant dessert which is one of our most popular with guests at home or at Rapallo.*

Place nuts on a large plate and stir in the sugar. Form mascarpone into balls the size of a golf ball (1½ ounce) and set gently on the plate. Roll mascarpone in the nuts to cover and place 2 balls per serving on dessert plates. (The balls can be refrigerated up to 4 hours. Bring to room temperature before serving.)

To serve gently pour 1 tablespoon of Frangelico on each plate. Garnish with fresh mint.

Makes 8 servings.

1 cup toasted, peeled and finely ground hazelnuts
1 Tb. superfine sugar
12 ounces mascarpone cheese
½ cup Frangelico Liquore

Strawberries with Balsamic Vinegar

*O*nce we served this very traditional preparation of straw-berries at Rapallo. A bowl was ordered by customers vis-iting from Italy. At first glance of the dessert they said, "You know, in Italy we would serve this with black pepper." The waiter stayed while they sampled their dish and watched wide smiles appear as they discovered the black pepper. They ordered another bowl.

2 pints ripe
   strawberries
2 Tb. balsamic vinegar
2 Tb. sugar
½ tsp. freshly ground
   black pepper

Hull the strawberries and slice in half. Place all ingredients in a medium bowl and toss to coat the strawberries evenly. Divide the berries among 6 serving bowls or glasses or put in a large glass bowl. Pour the balsamic over them.

Makes 6 servings.

Orange and Asti Spumante Zabaglione

Zabaglione, a classic Italian dessert, is a wine custard made with marsala. Here we serve it cold, made with Asti Spumante instead of marsala and highlighted with orange juice. We use bottled orange juice because it has a more consistent and concentrated flavor than fresh.

Remove orange skin in long, thin strips using a zester. In a small saucepan bring 1 cup water to a boil. Add zest, simmer for 3 minutes and drain. Set aside.

In the saucepan bring ½ cup water and ½ cup of the sugar to a boil. Add zest, reduce and simmer for 5 minutes. Remove zest, spread out on a plate and cool to room temperature.

Combine egg yolks, Asti Spumante and remaining ¼ cup sugar in the top of a double boiler over simmering water. Do not let the water touch the top pan. Whisk vigorously until it is thick, frothy and smooth, about 5 minutes.

Remove from heat and gently stir in the orange juice. In a separate bowl whip the cream to soft peaks. Whisk ¼ of the cream into the zabaglione to lighten it, then gently fold in remaining cream until smooth.

Pour into 6 dessert cups or glasses. Gently place candied orange zest on top. Chill until set, about 1 hour. (Can be stored, covered and refrigerated, for up to 4 hours.)

Makes 6 servings.

1 orange
1½ cups water
¾ cup sugar
5 egg yolks
¼ cup Asti Spumante
½ cup bottled orange juice
1 cup heavy cream

Peaches in Parchment

*C*ooking in parchment, "al cartoccio," seals in the steam *and flavors during cooking so that the aroma bursts out when you tear open the parchment. This is an excellent way to use peaches that are not quite ripe.*

**6 peaches, each cut into
  12 slices**
3 Tb. sugar
**¼ cup Amaretto
  Liquore**
**6 Tb. chopped almonds,
  toasted**

Preheat oven to 375°F.

Cut six 12-inch squares of parchment paper (you can also use unwaxed butcher paper or aluminum foil). Fold papers in half and then unfold. For each square, place 12 peach slices in a single layer above the fold line (fig. 1). Sprinkle each with 1½ teaspoons sugar, 2 teaspoons Amaretto, and 1 tablespoon almonds. Fold paper over the peach to enclose. Turn the lower right hand corner over to form a right angle (fig. 2) then continue turning over the edge, crimping every inch, to form a tight plaited seal (fig. 3). Twist the end to "lock" (fig. 4). Put on a cookie sheet and cook for 8 to 12 minutes or until the parchment has puffed up. Serve at once in the parchment.

Makes 6 servings.

1. Placing peach slices above fold in parchment.
2. Folding corner of parchment to make a right angle.
3. Folding the edge of the parchment to seal.
4. Twisting the end of the parchment.

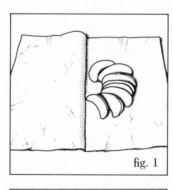

fig. 1

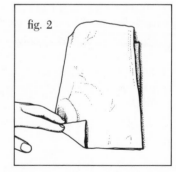

fig. 2

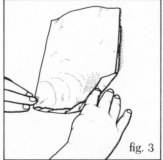

fig. 3

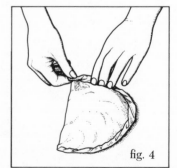

fig. 4

Cappuccino Creams

These custards are very smooth and creamy. You can also use freshly brewed espresso though we have found that coffee crystals give a consistent result.

Preheat oven to 325°F.

In a medium saucepan combine the cream and dissolved coffee. Heat over medium-high to just below boiling and remove. In a medium bowl stir the sugar into the yolks until well blended. With a wooden spoon slowly add the hot cream mixture into the yolks, stirring constantly to avoid curdling the yolks. Add the salt. Divide the mixture evenly between 6 cappuccino cups or individual souffle cups.

Place cups in an ovenproof pan and pour boiling water around them to reach halfway up the sides of the cups. Cover loosely with foil and bake for 50 to 60 minutes or until the edges are just set. Remove the cups and refrigerate until chilled. (Creams can be stored, covered and refrigerated, for 24 hours.)

Serve creams in their cups with crunchy cookies or biscotti.

Makes 6 servings.

2 cups heavy cream
2 Tb. instant coffee crystals, dissolved in ⅓ cup boiling water
½ cup plus 2 Tb. sugar
4 egg yolks
Pinch of salt

Granita

Granita is a coarse-textured shaved ice. Traditionally eaten as a mid-day refresher it is also a perfect light ending to a meal. Granita is very easy to make, requiring no special equipment. Here are two of our favorite recipes, highlighting the strong flavors of lemon and Chianti.

LEMON AND BASIC GRANITA

¾ cup sugar
1½ cups water
¾ cup plus 2 Tb. fresh lemon juice (about ¾ pound lemons)
3 large basil leaves

In a small saucepan heat the sugar and water until the sugar is dissolved. Let cool. Add the lemon juice. Cut basil leaves crosswise into thin strips. Add to the lemon juice. Pour into a large shallow baking pan and put in the freezer. When ice crystals start to form (usually a couple hours) stir the mixture from side to side every 20 minutes. When thoroughly frozen mound the granita in dessert glasses and garnish with fresh basil. (Can be stored, covered, in the freezer up to 1 week.)
Makes 3 cups.

CHIANTI GRANITA

4 cups Chianti (red wine)
1 cup sugar

In a small saucepan, bring the wine and sugar to a boil and gently boil for 5 minutes to dissipate the alcohol. Cool.
Pour in a large shallow baking pan and put in the freezer. When ice crystals start to form (usually a couple of hours) stir the mixture from side to side every 20 minutes. When thoroughly frozen mound the granita in dessert glasses. (Can be stored in the freezer for up to 1 week.)
Makes 3 cups.

The Aperitivo

The aperitivo (aperitivi, plural) like its more familiar French cousin, aperitif, comes from the Latin verb *aperire*, meaning "to open"—to open the evening and set the mood, to open the taste buds for what's to come. Hard alcohol may numb the palate but wines and aperitivi were made to be enjoyed with food. Aperitivi and other starters come in endless varieties and combinations. Try some of our favorite aperitivi listed in this chapter or invent some of your own. To help you with this we've included a little background on Italian wines and aperitivi.

The best known aperitivo is vermouth. Vermouth has a history going back as far as ancient Palestinian records. Today, vermouth is processed in three basic styles: rosso (sweet red), bianco (sweet white), and secco (dry white). They are made from simple wines flavored with some 50 herbal and aromatic extracts, then sweetened and fortified. Some principal flavorings are wormwood (from which the word vermouth is derived), hyssop, ginger, juniper, clove, orange, horehound and especially quinine which gives vermouth its characteristic bitter flavor. Italian vermouths, made mostly around Turin, are a little sweeter than their French counterparts. In Italy they are always served well chilled over cracked ice or with the addition of soda water or orange juice. The leading producers are Martini and Rossi, Cinzano, Gancia, Cora, Barbera and Riccadonna. Open bottles will keep several months in the refrigerator.

Two widely known aperitivi are Campari and Punt e Mes, both produced in Milan. Campari is a blend of herbs, orange peel and quinine, and is a bright deep-red color. It is served over ice with mixers to soften its bitterness. Punt e Mes is more bittersweet and light caramel in color. It is served chilled and usually mixed with orange juice. The name comes from a Milanese stockbroker's term meaning "a point and a half" which is said to be how the business clientele liked their drinks mixed.

Bitters, such as Angostura and Carpano, are a holdover from the Middle Ages when they were used as medicine. Medieval pharmacology recognized hundreds of flavorings extracted from fruits and aromatics in an alcohol base, as many essences were not water soluble. As in medieval times they are used today as digestives or, in the case of Frenet-branca, a hang-over cure. Every Italian bar stocks numerous bitters to be served with ice and soda as an aperitivo or after dinner as a *digestivo*. We Americans more commonly use them as a flavoring in mixed drinks.

Wine is often the most familiar of the aperitivi. On many occasions with friends in Lodi, 40 miles from Milan, we have enjoyed a simple white wine and shavings of Parmesan cheese. This simple way to begin the evening occurs throughout Italy. Italians would never drink a robust wine with antipasti. We also follow this practice when choosing California wines. Light and medium-bodied varietals, such as chenin blanc, fume blanc and California gamay, are good matches for the varied flavors and textures of an antipasto table. A menu of grilled dishes calls for a light chardonnay or a fruity zinfandel. A picnic or warm weather menu needs a refreshing rosé, gewurztraminer or reisling.

Italy produces not only more wine but more wine varieties than any other country. Some bottles are produced from a single grape variety, many are blends, such as Chianti. Most of the lower quality wine is sold within Italy or to neighboring European countries as blending wines. As the United States imports more wine from Italy than any other country, the Italian government is interested in protecting this market by exporting only high quality wines. In 1963 Italy passed its famous wine law *Denominazione di origine,* to protect the quality and genuineness of Italy's better wines. It established a committee to uphold strict standards of labeling, wine making and even vineyard production levels. Wines to be exported to the United States must pass government tests for quality and are granted the *Marchio Nazionale,* which appears on the bottle's neck band as a red seal reading "I.N.E.". The wine's name of origin and the characteristics attached to the name are further protected by controlled denomination of origin (D.O.C.) appearing on a label.

Virtually all Italian white wines are well suited to antipasti and should be uncorked while young and fresh. Good antipasto reds include Bardolino, Valpolicella, Chianti, Dolcetto, Nebbiolo and Sangiovese. Robust reds such as Barolo, Barbera d'Asti and Barberesco are better suited to richer, heavier meals.

Sparkling wines signify festiveness and celebration, and are well matched with a variety of foods. Of course French Champagne is always delightful but carries a stiff price tag. We have found some fine, less expensive alternatives from Italy and Spain. Both California and New York produce fine sparkling wines that are often stronger and sharper than comparably priced Spanish and Italian sparkling wines; but for the most part they are not as well made in the inexpensive catagories.

For dry sparkling wines below $10, look to the Spanish imports. Much of the vineyards are in the Northern Penedas area of Catalonia where they produce more sparkling wine than the Champagne region of France. Made from local xarel-lo, macabeo and parellada grapes, these sparkling wines are often made in the same *methode champenoise* as French Champagne but are slightly sweeter. The largest sparkling wine producer, Cordorniu, reputedly has the most extensive underground cellars in the world, 11 miles in 5 tiers. Together with Freixenet they produce 75% of the sparkling wines from their region. Other notable houses are Segura Viudas, Rene Barbier and Marques de Monistrol. It is interesting to note that Freixenet recently released Gloria Ferrer (their new sparkling wine from Sonoma, California, priced around $10) which outshines many higher priced Californians.

Italy produces a sweet sparkling wine for under $10, Asti Spumante. The fruity Asti is produced near the town of the same name in Piedmont and is made from muscat grapes. These wines are made by the charmant process which helps capture the fragrance of the grape and produces a low alcohol, fresh, fruity wine. They are often served well chilled with a few drops of bitters or Italian syrups. Several of the large Asti Spumante importers, Grancia, Martini and Rossi, and Cinzano, are also producing high-quality dry sparkling wines called "premium spumante" or simply "spumante", which are just now becoming available in the United States.

Italy also produces world class dry sparkling wines by *metodo classico (methode champenoise)*. These wines come from the Northern Trentino-Alto Adige and Lombardy areas where the cooler climates produce chardonnay, pinot and riesling grapes that have a high acidity and neutral character coveted by the great champagne houses of France. Premium spumantes are softer, slightly less acidic than the French wines and are lighter and drier than the Spanish. The best premium spumantes available here come from Ferrari, Ca'del Bosco, Villa Banfi, Berlucchi and Equipe trentina Spumanti. They sell for $10 to $20.

Setting up an Aperitivo Bar

When choosing components for the bar consider the number of guests there will be and any idea you might have of their tastes. You will want to expand your offerings for larger groups. It is fun to assign an enthusiastic friend to tend bar and encourage your guests to experiment with different combinations.

For up to 15 people:

Have a red and white wine, a white vermouth, a lager style beer, campari, soda water, orange juice and fresh lemons for twists. Choose a couple of recipes from this chapter and have those ingredients on hand.

For groups larger than 15:

Add 1 or 2 sparkling wines (Spanish or Californian and an Asti Spumante), red vermouth, Punt e Mes, a dark full-bodied beer, a non-alcoholic varietal grape juice, Angostura bitters, Rose's lime juice, fresh fruit, Italian syrups in several flavors, and any ingredients needed for additional aperitivo recipes.

Equipment for a full bar should include measuring spoons, 1-ounce measuring jigger, long handled spoon, bottle openers, corkscrews, ice tongs, ice bucket, cracked ice, zester, small knife, cutting board, towels, cocktail napkins, and copies of the recipes. You should have 3 types of glasses: tall (Tom Collins), short (Old Fashion) and wine.

Set up the bar next to refrigeration if possible, or have buckets full of ice to chill the bottles. The items to be chilled are white and sparkling wines, beers, vermouths, Campari, Punt e Mes, soda water and orange juice. Keep red wines, bitters and syrups at room temperature.

TIPS

- Never use bottled lemon juice as the preservatives kill the flavor.
- Use the freshest ingredients and fruits as possible.
- Oranges are so variable in quality, however, that bottled juice or concentrate might be preferable to pale, juiceless oranges. Sample the oranges before you use them.
- Do not cut the lemon or orange slices thinner than ¼ inch or they will curl.
- When sugar is called for, use "superfine".
- A dash is ⅙ teaspoon.
- Stir drinks thoroughly when called for.
- For mixed drinks pour the alcoholic liquids in the glass first.
- Soda water refers to your choice of sparkling or mineral waters, seltzers or club soda.

Summer Frost

2 Tb. superfine sugar
1¼ ounces pineapple
  juice
3 ounces Asti Spumante
Dash bitters
Crushed ice

Pour the sugar onto a plate. Moisten the rim of a tall glass with a little pineapple juice and dip the glass into the sugar to frost the glass. Add the other ingredients, stir and add crushed ice to fill the glass.

Torino Lemonade

Juice of 1 lemon
¼ cup Secco (dry white
  vermouth)
2 tsp. superfine sugar
½ cup crushed ice
¼ cup soda water
2 Tb. superfine sugar,
  for rim
Lime wedge

In a cocktail shaker or covered jar place lemon juice, Secco, 2 teaspoons sugar and ice. Shake vigorously for 5 seconds. Add soda. Place 2 tablespoons of sugar on a plate. Moisten the rim of a wine glass and twirl in the sugar to form a sugar rim. Pour lemonade into the glass. Squeeze and drop the lime into the glass.

White Wine Cooler

½ cup white wine
½ tsp. Punt e Mes
1 tsp. Torani raspberry
  syrup
¼ cup soda water
Crushed ice
Fresh strawberries

Pour liquids into a wine glass. Stir well and add crushed ice to fill the glass. Garnish with fresh strawberries.

Campari Orange Blush

Pour liquids into a wine glass, stir well and add crushed ice to fill.

1 ounce Campari
¼ cup orange juice
Crushed ice

Merry Widow

This is an adaptation of a traditional drink using both Italian and Spanish wines.

Pour liquids and orange twist into a wine glass, stir well and add crushed ice to fill.

1½ ounces Rosso (sweet
   red vermouth)
1½ ounces Amontillado
   sherry
Orange twist
Crushed ice

Sour Widow

Sour Widow is a variation of the Merry Widow that has a nice lemony flavor.

Pour liquids and citrus slices in a tall glass, stir well and add crushed ice to fill.

3 ounces fino sherry
1½ ounces Rosso (sweet
   red vermouth)
1½ ounces lemonade
¼ tsp. grenadine or
   marichino syrup
1 slice lemon
1 slice orange
Crushed ice

Cranberry-Pineapple Cocktail

2 ounces cranberry
   juice
2 ounces pineapple juice
2 tsp. Punt e Mes
Crushed ice

Pour liquids into a short glass, stir well and add crushed ice to fill.

Light Negroni

We've lightened this classic drink by adding more soda. This version is more suited to food but still retains its characteristic bitterness.

1 ounce gin
1 ounce Campari
1 ounce Rosso (sweet
   red vermouth)
4 ounces soda water
Crushed ice
Lemon twist

Pour liquids into a tall glass, stir well and add crushed ice to fill. Garnish with lemon twist.

Asti Albicocca

We developed this for a New Year's Eve dinner at Rapallo. Every diner started the celebration with this festive drink.

4 ounces Asti Spumante
1 tsp. apricot brandy
4 drops Torani apricot
   syrup
Lemon twist

Pour ingredients into a champagne glass and stir.

Asti Spumante Cocktails

Pour 6 ounces of Asti Spumante in a wine glass and add one of the following:
- splash of Punt e Mes
- splash of Campari
- 2 dashes bitters
- splash of Torani raspberry syrup, dash of bitters and a lemon twist
- splash of Torani grenadine syrup and a lemon twist
- generous splash of Bianco (sweet white vermouth)
- splash of Sambuca with lots of fresh fruit wedges such as tangerines, pineapple, lime and berries

Sicilian Sangria

Mix all ingredients in a large punch bowl.
    Makes six 8-ounce servings

Variations: For a fruitier punch add one ounce of any Torani syrup. For a stronger punch add more marsala. Add soda (about 1 part soda to 3 parts punch) to each glass for a lighter, spritzier sangria. Also try adding strawberries, cherries or peach slices.

1 bottle red wine
1 cup marsala
1 cup orange juice
1 cup pineapple juice
1 lemon, sliced
1 lime, sliced
1 orange, sliced

Grape and Lime Crush

Pour liquids over crushed ice in a tall glass and garnish with a lime slice.

3 ounces grape juice
Juice of ½ lime
2 dashes bitters (more if desired)
1 ounce soda water
Crushed ice
Slice of lime

Italian Soda

4 ounces soda water
1 Tb. Torani syrup of
   any flavor
1 dash bitters
Crushed ice

Pour liquids over crushed ice in a tall glass.

Sambuca Julep

*S*ambuca is an anise (licorice) flavored sweet liquore from
Rome. It is delightful in combination with pineapple and
mint. Here's an Italian version of a Southern favorite.

5 mint leaves
Crushed ice
1 ounce Sambuca
2 ounces pineapple juice
4 drops mint extract
1 large sprig of mint,
   for garnish

Put mint leaves and crushed ice in a tall glass. Add liquids
and mix well. Garnish with mint sprig.

Designing an Antipasto Feast

One of the advantages of these antipasto-style dishes is that they are flexible and versatile. Lighter ones can be served as first courses and heartier dishes as entrees, as in a typical American meal. Or serve them all at once for the feel of a real antipasto table. Combining dishes forms interesting interplay of different and similar elements.

When planning a menu the first consideration is what ingredients are available. What is fresh and in season? We cook according to the market, as the Italians do, by choosing whatever is at its peak.

Next look for contrast in taste, appearance and texture. When choosing a very soft textured dish—such as Marinated Mozzarella—serve something crunchy—perhaps Pasta Fries. The creamy texture of Garlic Bread Custards is nicely contrasted by the crisp snap of raw vegetables in Beets and Cucumbers with Gorgonzola. We also look for a simple, straightforward taste to set off a more complex recipe. It is easier on the cook, too, preparing only one complicated recipe. With the Coniglio Farcito (Stuffed Rabbit) you need the simple clarity of a dish like Figs, Prosciutto and Mint. Rich pâté style dishes need some acidity to cut their palate coating qualities. For example, with Chicken Salami serve Pickled Eggplant. One of our favorite antipasti combinations is the pairing of sweet and salty. We serve sweet Sicilian-style tuna (Caponatuna) with a dish with the natural saltiness of prosciutto such as Grilled Radicchio and Prosciutto. And we also look for the interplay of colors. The monochromatic earthtoned Panzarotti (ham and cheese filled pastries) benefit from the colorful Sweet Pickled Vegetables.

The size and type of gathering also helps determine the menu. For a get together with a few friends choose 4 or 5 dishes, some hot and some room temperature. If you are sitting at a table choose foods that are appropriate for a sit-down dinner, such as Ragu di Tonno (Tuna Ragout) or Two-Pesto Polenta Torta. If you are gathering around the fire choose simple, hand-held foods.

For a larger gathering choose a variety of recipes. Include nibbling food and more substantial dishes. They can be set out on the table before guests arrive, freeing the cook to enjoy the party. We like to serve a hot dish every 30 minutes or so, adding new interest to the table. And as the evening winds down present 1 or 2 dolci.

A "happy hour" party should center around the aperitivo bar. Choose a few of the hand-held dishes that are perfect to nibble on with drinks, such as Crostini, Fried Chick-peas and Pasta Fries.

No matter what type or size of feast, the bar helps set the theme and complements the food. Aperitivi and wines, as much as anything, make a party interesting and unique. Set up an aperitivo bar and encourage guests to have fun mixing their own aperitivi.

Use the menus we've sketched to get started, but let your tastes guide you to design antipasto feasts of your own.

COOK'S NOTE

The recipes for the dishes in our menus can be found by looking up the recipe title in the index.

Winter Evening Buffet

This buffet is perfect for holiday entertaining. It is a diverse and elegant menu, full of intriguing tastes—garlic, spices, mint, prosciutto, sun-dried tomatoes—and a complexity of textures. The dishes are mostly done ahead with only the polenta torta requiring last minute assembly. This rich hearty food is perfect for chilly evenings.

Stuffed Breast of Veal with Garlic Mayonnaise

Onions filled with Sweet Lamb Sausage

Two-Pesto Polenta Torta

Garlic Bread Custards

Beets and Cucumbers with Gorgonzola

Fennel Seed Crackers

Spiced Walnuts

Cappuccino Creams

Oranges with Amontillado Sherry

Outdoor Grill Party

The star of the party is the grill. Grilling in the open air is as popular in Italy as it is here. This menu features dishes that are not typical barbecue fare. It is a fun, relaxing party since most of the work is done ahead.

Pumpkin Seed Dip

Pasta Fries

Panzanella

Pickled Eggplant

Grilled Chard and Fontina Packets

Calamari with Balsamic Marinade

Grilled Radicchio and Prosciutto

Involtini di Vitella

Lemon and Basil Granita

Seafood of Venice

Venice, the city of canals, is famous for its wonderful seafood. This menu combines four different types of seafood—prawns paired with Grappa (a white brandy from north of Venice), scallops prepared in a Venetian style traditionally made with sole, broiled mussels and marinated calamari. A rice frittata and a refreshing salad of fennel and apples balances the table.

Prawns in Grappa and Orange

Scallops in Saor

Calamari and Celery Salad

Broiled Mussels

Arborio Rice Frittata

Fennel and Apple Salad with Poppy Seeds

Spiced Walnuts

Country Picnic

This is no ordinary picnic. Our "al fresco" menu is based on standard picnic food—chicken, sliced meats, crackers—but with an Italian flair. Everything packs well and is easy to carry.

Chicken Salami

Sweet Pickled Vegetables

Crostini with Budino di Fegato

Ricotta and Feta Torta

Duck Breast Prosciutto

Gorgonzola Domes

Greens with Extra Virgin Olive Oil and Lemon Juice
(tossed at the picnic site)

Parmigiano Reggiano with Walnuts

Fresh Fruit

Informal Gathering of Friends

This menu is composed of simple recipes that are quick to prepare. Marinated Mozzarella and Pickled Garlic can be kept on hand, ready for unexpected get togethers. Several of the dishes can be hand-held, perfect for an informal gathering.

Frittata di Pasta

Fennel and Apple Salad with Poppy Seeds

Marinated Mozzarella

Amalfi-style Sandwiches

Fish Spiedini with Pickled Garlic

Figs, Prosciutto and Mint

Roman Feast

Suppli di Riso, eggplants and peppers, figs with prosciutto and mint, and marinated mozzarella are typical antipasti served in the trattorias of Rome. We have added dishes that feature ingredients often found on the menus of elegant Roman restaurants, rabbit and crab. Plan this menu for the fall when crabs, figs, fennel and peppers are in season.

Coniglio Farcito

Figs, Prosciutto and Mint

Suppli di Riso

Marinated Mozzarella

Sweet Pickled Vegetables

Bacon-wrapped Fennel

Crab with Oregano Marinade

Roasted Eggplants and Peppers

Sicilian Lunch

This menu is based on the bold and lively flavors of Sicily. We use ingredients indicative of the cuisine of the island: tuna, green tomatoes, pine nuts and goat cheese.

Involtini di Vitella

Capona-tuna

Green Tomatoes Fried with Basil

Sfincione—topped with a Sicilian goat- or sheep-milk cheese

Apricots with Biscotti and Pine nut Filling

Midnight Supper for Two

This is a romantic and elegant light supper that requires very little last minute attention. Serve this menu in the spring when green beans and peaches are at their best. Prepare half of each recipe for a supper for two.

Sambuca Prawns with Prosciutto

Green Beans with Orange Rouille

Sweet Lamb Sausage Bread

Peaches in Parchment

Asti Spumante

Index